USAIN BOLT

MIKE ROWBOTTOM is a freelance journalist who writes widely on sport, and whose current job titles include chief features writer on www.insidethegames. biz. He also writes regularly for *Rowing & Regatta*, the British rowing magazine, and covers athletics for the International Association of Athletics Federations, and the Samsung Diamond League website. Mike has covered the last five Summer Olympics and four Winter Olympics for the *Independent*, for which he wrote a weekly humorous column for seven years. He has also worked for the *Daily Mail*, the *Observer*, *The Times*, the *Guardian* and the *Sunday Correspondent*. He co-authored the autobiography of Olympic 400 metres silver medallist Roger Black, entitled *How Long's The Course?* (Andre Deutsch, 1997)

USAIN BOLT
Fast As Lightning

MIKE ROWBOTTOM

Arcadia Books Ltd
15–16 Nassau Street
London W1W 7AB

www.arcadiabooks.com

First published by BlackAmber Inspirations,
an imprint of Arcadia Books 2010

Series Editor: Rosemarie Hudson
Copyright Mike Rowbottom © 2010

A catalogue record for this book is available from the British Library.

ISBN 978-1-906413-82-8

Typeset in Minion by MacGuru Ltd
Printed and bound in the United Kingdom by CPI Cox & Wyman, Reading, RG1 8EX

Arcadia Books gratefully acknowledges the financial support of Arts Council England.

Arcadia Books supports PEN, the fellowship of writers who work together to promote
literature and its understanding. English PEN upholds writers' freedoms in Britain and
around the world, challenging political and cultural limits on free expression.
To find out more, visit *www.englishpen.org* or contact
English PEN, 6–8 Amwell Street, London EC1R 1UQ

Arcadia Books distributors are as follows:

in the UK and elsewhere in Europe:
Turnaround Publishers Services
Unit 3, Olympia Trading Estate

Jacana Media (Pty) Ltd
PO Box 291784
Melville 2109
Johannesburg

Arcadia Books is the *Sunday Times* Small Publisher of the Year

Contents

Foreword

By Dame Kelly Holmes, MBE,
Double Olympic Champion

MIKE ROWBOTTOM HAS WRITTEN about me since I started my senior international career in athletics in 1993, and has witnessed many of my highs and my lows, my tears and my triumphs. He saw me pull up injured in my 1500 metres heat when I was the favourite to win at the 1997 World Championships in Athens, and he was in Budapest seven years later when I was tripped and fell as I went for what would have been my first global gold at the World Indoor Championships.

He was there in 2002 when I won the Commonwealth title for a second time in front of that unforgettable home crowd in Manchester, and at the Athens Olympics two years later when I won my 800/1500 metres double.

When I retired from the sport in 2005 I put Mike on my 'podium' of writers for the articles he had done about me for the *Independent*. Since then, for insidethegames.biz, he has continued to cover a huge amount of my work including my mentoring initiative 'On Camp With Kelly', the establishment of my charity, the Dame Kelly Holmes Legacy Trust, and my role as the president of Commonwealth Games England.

Given my Jamaican heritage, albeit very distant from anything I know, I was particularly interested to read the chapter dealing with that country's rich running tradition, and to see where Usain Bolt fitted into it. Over the last two years, Usain has literally exploded into the forefront of everyone's mind, becoming a massively popular figure in world athletics and sport, both because of his astounding sprint performances and his lively and high-spirited personality. But he has not been an overnight sensation – he has had his struggles to get to where he is, and I can identify very well with the frustration that must have caused him.

There are only moments in history that we sit up and take note of amazing events and for the sport of athletics it is great to have an athlete like Usain realising his talents, and this book offers some fascinating insights into his character, his development and his future potential.

1

Big in Beijing

THE ELECTRONICALLY ENHANCED SOUND of a starting pistol reverberates around the Bird's Nest stadium in Beijing, and the 2008 Olympic 100 metres final is underway. For the 100,000 spectators packed into the intricately wrought arena, and a worldwide TV audience of 178 million, this is the high point of the first Saturday night of athletics at the Games. Earlier in the evening they have seen the previous year's world 100 metres champion, Tyson Gay, whose preparations for the Games have been affected by injury, knocked out in the semi-final. Which means that only one man, Asafa Powell, is likely to stand between the Olympic gold medal and the fellow Jamaican getting into his stride three lanes inside him. At 6ft 2in tall, Powell is a broad, powerful athlete – the kind of athlete who has been winning the Olympic 100 metres title since the post-war Games resumed in London in 1948. And he has used that physique to good effect in the previous three years, setting world records of 9.77 seconds and 9.74 seconds.

But the man in lane four – Usain Bolt – looks a different kind of runner.

He's tall – in fact, at 6ft 5in he is too tall for 100 metres sprinting according to conventional coaching. Even his own coach, Glen Mills, has suggested that his long legs and frame are better suited to longer events such as the 200 or 400 metres, as it takes him so long to 'unfurl' himself out of the blocks. Bolt has already confounded traditional coaching theory, however, by reducing Powell's record to 9.72 seconds at a meeting held two months before the Beijing Games. And in only his fifth serious race at the distance. Freaky. So the question being asked as the Olympics got underway was: is this a Bolt that is going to strike more than once in the same place?

The 21-year-old's performance in the earlier rounds has already indicated the answer to that question. After jogging home in his quarter-final in a time of 9.92 seconds – a world record just 20 years earlier – he had announced laconically: 'I just ran the first 50 metres. Then I looked around to make sure I was safe and I shut off.' The words, by themselves, suggest arrogance. And yet their delivery, with a disarming smile, renders them charming.

Before the start of an Olympic 100 metres final there is usually an extraordinary state of tension among the competitors. Unlike World Cup finalists, the men who gather for this four-yearly contest know they have around 10 seconds to justify their sporting existence. The sprinters pace up and down, some deliberately glaring at their opponents, others deliberately avoiding any other's gaze. They shake out their limbs, already warmed and prepared, as if one final shake will make them faster.

What they don't do is play around. And yet this is what Bolt does. As the runners are announced, he does a little dance – it later turns out to be one of his favourite moves from the Jamaican dancehall scene that he loves so much. And when it is his turn to have his name read out, he breaks out into a broad grin and assumes the archer-like stance that is to become his 'Lightning Bolt' trademark – left arm outstretched with index finger pointing towards the sky, right arm drawn back as if pulling on the string of a bow – before firing a make-believe arrow into the tumult around him.

Bolt's start in the final does not appear exceptional, an impression later confirmed by the release of his reaction time to the gun – at 0.165 seconds, he is the second slowest in the field of eight. At the 30 metres mark, he is no more than a more easily visible bobbing head among many, with Richard

Thompson, of Trinidad and Tobago, slightly ahead of the field. But what happens in the next 50 metres is astonishing. There is a sound that goes through huge sporting crowds when something extraordinary happens. When Zinedine Zidane volleys a goal for Real Madrid from outside the penalty. When Muhammad Ali comes off the ropes to down the giant, hitherto oppressive figure of George Foreman. When Michael Johnson wins the Olympic 200 metres title in 19.32 seconds. 19.32 seconds! And that is the sound which surges within the Bird's Nest stadium on this humid night as the man who stands head and shoulders above the rest translates superior height into superior speed.

By the 80 metres mark, the wave of runners who have been accompanying Bolt are now the wave behind as his sustained speed takes him into his own space. He is running free, out on his own, a clear and compelling spectacle. After glancing across to his right, where the figure of his friend Powell might conceivably be, but isn't, he switches from being a runner to being a celebrant. With 20 metres remaining, his arms drop down to his sides. Ten metres further on, he leans backwards and thumps his right hand onto his heart. Crossing the line, his face split by a grin, his energy overwhelms him and he carries on running and bounding his way round towards the back straight. The noise in the Bird's Nest reverberates in the ear. It's one of those moments. And all those present witness it, and always will have witnessed it ...

But for the first time in a little more than ten seconds, the tall figure in the yellow and green of Jamaica is no longer the centre of attention. That is now the digital clock standing at the finish line, which has this figure on it: 9.68 – very soon adjusted to its official mark of 9.69. It's the first 100 metres race to be run in under 9.70 seconds without a following wind exceeding the sport's allowable limit for record purposes of 2.00 metres per second. And all around the stadium, all around the world, people are saying the same thing: 'How fast could he run if he really tried?' Or even: 'How fast could he run if he really tried and he didn't have one of his laces undone?'

At the 1924 Olympics in Paris, the great Finnish middle-distance runner, Paavo Nurmi, won the double of 1500 metres and 5000 metres titles in the space of an hour, taking the first of them with such ease that one writer observed that he was 'probably the only man ever who has been able to slow down on purpose in the Olympic Games.'

Eighty-four years later the Olympic Games has witnessed another man with the ability to slow down to an Olympic gold medal. But slowing down in the 1500 metres is one thing; slowing down in the 100 metres quite another. The responses of Bolt's fellow runners pretty much cover the dominant emotions of the moment. They convey wonder – and doubt. The wondrousness is self-evident. The doubt an inevitable postscript to an event which has been tarnished periodically by doping abuse since the 1988 Seoul Olympics, where the Canadian, Ben Johnson, was infamously stripped of his 100 metres gold medal and world record of 9.79 seconds after testing positive for the banned steroid, stanozolol.

Since that traumatic sequence of events, the question asked, either explicitly or implicitly, of the fastest man or woman on earth, has always been the same one. And the answer has not always been satisfactory. 'It was good to be part of history,' Thompson tells reporters in the stadium's mixed zone. 'It is great for him and great for me to be right behind him. I don't think anyone was going to compete with him when he runs like that. I could see him slowing down and I was still pumping to the line. He's a phenomenal athlete. People think you have to be short, strong and stocky to be a great sprinter and Usain Bolt has defied that. It's the beginning of something else.'

Powell has been unable once again to find his most telling form at the crucial moments and is shocked and dismayed at finishing only fifth. But his assessment of his fellow countryman is generous: 'He's the best,' Powell says. 'There's no stopping him. He could have been faster.' Darvis Patton, who has finished eighth, insists everyone was overwhelmed by Bolt.

'It's not even close,' says the US sprinter. 'It's everybody catching up with Usain Bolt. He's a legend in his own right. The guy's a phenomenal athlete. He's a freak of nature.'

And so to the post-race press conference, where the character so evident in the grand arena shines through with every response. The convention for such occasions is to have the winner sitting with second- and third-placed athletes either side of him. Never can an Olympic silver and bronze medallist have felt more surplus to requirements.

As he waits for the cascade of questions that are about to pour over him from a room packed to the four walls with the world's press, Bolt is without question the most relaxed person present. He chews on the energy bar that he had in his hand as he strolled in. Inevitably, he is asked how much faster he might have gone if he had pushed to the line. 'I have not seen the replays yet so I can't really say,' he responds. 'People have been saying I could have run 9.60 but I haven't seen the replays yet so I couldn't really comment on that.'

Then comes a more light-hearted request: 'Take us through the day of the world's fastest man. What did he have for breakfast?' 'I never had breakfast,' Bolt says, to general laughter. 'I woke up at like eleven o'clock, sat around and watched some TV, had lunch, some nuggets (yes, chicken nuggets), then I pretty much went back to my room, slept again, then went back and got some more nuggets. Then I came to the track.' More laughter.

But then Jamaica's first Olympic 100 metres champion shows that he is not heartless in his high spirits when the questioning turns to his underperforming compatriot. How is his performance going to hurt Asafa Powell emotionally? 'I can't say,' Bolt says. 'I know Asafa and he is a great athlete, we're friends. He had a rough season at the start of the season. He had a couple of injuries and I know next season he's going to be coming back storming.' And Tyson Gay, the world champion who was eliminated in the semifinals? 'I'm looking forward also to Tyson Gay – I'm looking forward to competing against these guys next season,' Bolt says, before confirming that he will be contesting the 200 metres, and, on the day after his 22nd birthday, the 4×100 metres relay. As for the celebration in the moment of victory, he maintains: 'It wasn't planned. I wasn't celebrating; I was excited.'

Bolt's performance in the short sprint is already starting to raise speculation that Johnson's monumental world 200 metres record, set at the 1996 Atlanta Olympics, might after all not last as long as Bob Beamon's world long jump mark of 8.90 metres at the 1968 Olympics in the thin air of Mexico, which was not bettered for 23 years. The next question to Bolt, who has always described the 200 metres as

his favourite event, is therefore obvious. Can he beat
Johnson's record here? 'I'm not really worried about
world records,' Bolt responds. 'My aim is just to
win. There's a lot more time to think about that.' He
adds that he had not been concerned about setting
a new world 100 metres record either. 'I wasn't worried about the world record,' he insists. 'I didn't even
know I'd got the world record until after I had finished my victory lap. One aim was to come here and
be Olympic champion and I did just that – and I am
happy about that. I didn't know I was going to run so
fast. But I came out to be a champion, and I was.'

A champion he is. But two more gold medals
beckon him before he leaves Beijing …

Four days later, we are back in the Bird's Nest stadium as Bolt takes to the track in an effort to earn
the title which it has been his ambition to win since
he started to show serious promise as a child – the
Olympic 200 metres. Having won the 100 metres
gold medal without testing the limits of his ability,
Bolt has reached the final of the longer sprint by
jogging through the rounds, ambling home with half
an eye on the big screen at the end of the stadium to
check his leeway on lesser mortals. One place inside
him, in lane four, is the bulky figure of the defending
Olympic champion, Shawn Crawford of the United
States. Observers of the sport expect the American
to do what he likes to do, namely to try and unnerve

his opposition by blasting his way round the curve. As the gun fires, however, it is Bolt who pulls away from the straining figure inside him. By the halfway point, as he enters the 100 metre straight, the new 100 metres champion has already made winning the race a formality.

But there is no repeat of his performance in the shorter sprint. With all opposition irrelevant and a second Olympic title assured, this 6ft 5in figure of power and leverage eschews all playfulness and show, grits his teeth, pumps his big fists up level with his ears and, wonder of wonders, actually dips through the line towards his rich reward – a world record. As the stadium booms with sound and wonder once again, it is hard to know which is the most arresting sight – the digital scoreboard stopped at 19.30, or the sight of Usain Bolt actually heaving for breath.

The birthday boy – Bolt will turn 22 at midnight – has clearly had it in mind to give himself an early present that he will cherish forever in the event which has been the receptacle for his dearest dreams since he was a teenager. After the race, Bolt verbalises what he has already made evident with every straining sinew: 'I told myself, "I'm going to leave everything on the track." I did just that.'

Twelve years earlier in the heavy heat of Atlanta, Johnson finished 0.36 seconds clear of his nearest rival, Namibia's Frankie Fredericks. Bolt's margin of victory is 0.52 seconds over Churandy Martina of the Netherlands Antilles, who is later disqualified for a lane violation along with the third-placed American, Wallace Spearmon.

As after the 100 metres, Bolt's competitors are left straining for words. 'It's mind-blowing,' says Christian Malcolm of Great Britain, whose seventh place turned into fifth once the disqualifications were announced. 'I hear he looked impressive, but I didn't really get to see.' And so the comparisons begin. Bolt is the first man to hold Olympic 100 and 200 metres titles since Carl Lewis achieved the feat at the 1984 Los Angeles Games. He is the first to hold world records at 100 and 200 metres since his fellow Jamaican Don Quarrie was joint holder of the old, hand-timed marks of 9.9 seconds and 19.8 seconds in 1976, the year he won the 200 metres in Montreal to become the first man from his country to win an Olympic track title.

Most resonantly, Bolt has broken a record which many observers believed would stand for 30 years. 'Everything came together tonight,' Bolt concludes. 'I just blew my mind. And I blew the world's mind.' He has also, clearly, blown the mind of Kim Collins, the 2003 world 100 metres champion from St Kitts and Nevis, who finished eighth and last and was elevated to sixth with the DQs: 'It's ridiculous,' Collins says to reporters after the race. 'I mean, come on. How fast can you go before records can't be broken? We thought the 100 record could possibly go to 9.6, but we never thought the 200 record could be broken. I didn't think it would happen while I was still running. How fast can a human being run before there is no more going fast?'

A year later, Bolt will have more to offer on that question. But now he is turning his attention to the last of his three events in the Chinese capital – the sprint relay. Meanwhile, the sound system inside the Bird's Nest is playing 'Happy Birthday' to the new champion – and the crowd is joining in … Bolt explains afterwards that speculation about whether he would have enough speed endurance to break the 200 as well as the 100 metres record is less relevant than it at first appears, as he has been working over 400 metres in training. It is a strategy that has paid off. 'When I was watching the replay I was looking at myself and going, "That guy's fast!"' he exclaims. 'A lot of people compare me to Michael Johnson but I don't compare myself to a lot of other people because I'm trying to be just me. Michael is a great athlete and he revolutionised the sport. I just changed it a little bit.'

In the wake of Bolt's latest flourish, Johnson – the original Superman – has responded with uncharacteristic fervour. 'Simply incredible,' he tells BBC viewers. 'This guy is Superman II.' But this guy isn't having any of that. 'I'm Lightning Bolt,' he proclaims with a grin. And Lightning that is about to strike not twice, but three times in the same spot ...

It is a measure of the impact Jamaica's sprinters have made on the Olympics that the question before the 4×100 metres relay final is not who will win, but whether the quartet of Nesta Carter, Michael Frater, Bolt and Powell will break the world record of 37.40 seconds set by the United States team at the 1992 Barcelona Olympics, anchored by the predominant sprinter of his era, Carl Lewis, whose relatively tall, lean frame made him something of a precursor to Bolt among more squat, muscular types. The answer to that question arrives swiftly. In 37.10 seconds, to be precise, with Powell, taking the baton and a massive lead from Bolt, running the last leg hard all the way to the line in what later turns out to be the fastest recorded relay split of 8.70 seconds. So Powell has an Olympic gold at last, supercharged by the encouragement of his third-leg teammate, who follows him all the way down the final straight, yelling encouragement.

For the Americans, so long the dominating force in world sprinting, this is the last of a succession of blows to their confidence – or, as some in the Jamaican camp would have it, their arrogance. The Beijing Olympics have been a stunning triumph for Jamaican sprinting in general, and Usain Bolt in particular.

And inevitably, the comparisons with athletics' stellar performers of the past begin. Was this the greatest Olympic track athlete ever? How did Bolt match up to the great Olympic sprinters of the past, such as Jesse Owens, who won four golds at the 1936 Berlin Games, or Carl Lewis, who matched Owens' haul at the 1984 LA Games and subsequently added five more Olympic golds. One other factor which gets airplay is the relatively advanced age at which other outstanding sprinters have produced their best. Donovan Bailey had won his Olympic 100 metres gold in the world record time of 9.84 seconds at 29. Michael Johnson had been a month off the same age when he ran his 200 metres world record of 19.32. The implication is clear. Bolt's best is yet to come.

Meanwhile, he has the world's attention, as it is reported that for every Google search made over the previous weekend for Brad Pitt, Tom Cruise, Ronaldinho, David Beckham and Tiger Woods, there were 7.5 for Bolt. Bolt's victories have been watched on huge screens set up in Kingston's Mandela Park, prompting street parties which have gone on all night long. Sales of Usain Bolt watches, stamps and T-shirts boom. Another measure of Bolt's impact upon his sport occurs nine days after the Games have ended, when, at the Athletissima meeting in Lausanne, he wins the 200 metres in 19.63 seconds. It is a meeting record – but on the night, it is not Bolt's performance that is significant. That comes from Powell, who reduces his 100 metres personal best to 9.72 seconds, and merits only passing mentions in reports. Were it not for Bolt, Powell would now be established in his own illustrious space, 0.05 seconds faster than any other 100 metres sprinter, which is a very significant margin for the event. Were it not for Bolt ...

After finishing his season with another victory over Powell in Brussels, Bolt returns to Jamaica and is the main attraction of a motorcade which parades the newly returned Olympians through the packed streets of Kingston before depositing them at a sports gala held in their honour at a national stadium also heaving with supporters. The events form part of the government's homecoming celebrations for its Olympians. The Jamaicans have won 11 medals in Beijing – and so the celebrations are arranged over 11 days. Bolt is greeted by the Prime Minister, Bruce Golding, and awarded the Order of Distinction, Commander Rank by the Governor General, Professor Sir Kenneth Hall. The official trappings are now laden upon his athletic achievements ...

Bolt had arrived in Beijing as an established and potentially brilliant 200 metres runner who, rather surprisingly, had made an excursion into the shorter sprint that had earned him the world record two months before the Games got underway. While many experts took him to win the Olympic 200 metres, that judgement might not have been so clear had Gay, who had won the world 100 and 200 metres titles in Osaka the year before, not failed to qualify for the longer sprint in Beijing after suffering an injury at the unforgiving US trials, which historically offered championship places only to the first three runners home in each event, no matter what ill fortune might befall its finest performers. And while Bolt's vivid emergence in the 100 metres event to which his long legs and body were not supposed to be suited had established him as a likely Olympic gold medallist, there were still those who fancied victory lay within the span of either Gay or Powell. Gay had clearly struggled to regain full fitness after his hamstring injury, but the argument was put forward in more than one quarter that the rest may have been good for him, and that his failure to qualify for the 200 metres would allow him to devote all his energies to the 100 metres, where, during the US trials, he had recorded 9.68 seconds, albeit with a following wind of twice the allowable force for record purposes.

As for Powell, well, he had failed to deliver at the last Olympics, and in the subsequent two World Championships. But he had managed to take the Commonwealth title two years earlier, and more to the point, he had six of the fastest eight 100 metres times to his credit. If he could get his mind right, the thinking went, he could still show Bolt, whom he had beaten in Stockholm a month before the Games, that he would be better advised turning his attention back to the distance where he had always had the strongest ambition to succeed. But Bolt made all these calculations as nothing as he captivated Beijing, and the wider world, with his speed and exuberance. In the space of a week, he became the face of his sport; indeed, transcended his sport. The world, it seemed, could not get enough of this new, shining phenomenon.

And yet, as Bert Cameron, the Jamaican coach who won the first ever world 400 metres title in 1983, remarked in the wake of Bolt's opening flourish at the Games: 'We knew what was coming.' Bolt may have flashed onto the world's consciousness like lightning, but any Jamaican could have told you he was no bolt from the blue. From the first moment Usain Bolt became an athlete, it was clear that he could do something special. Jamaica had been awaiting his overnight success for almost a decade ...

2

Jamaica's Heritage

SPEAKING AT A PRESS CONFERENCE in Shanghai after
the second of the IAAF's Diamond League meetings,
Usain Bolt was asked to account for Jamaica's hugely
successful sprint performances in the most recent ver-
sions of the Olympic Games and World Championships. 'Most Asian people are very good at gymnastics
and stuff,' he said, a little uncomfortably. 'In Jamaica
we are good at running. That's pretty much it.' If the
most popular question at the 2008 Beijing Olympics
was 'How does Usain Bolt run so fast?' the second
most popular was: 'How do the Jamaicans run so fast?'

A large part of the answer to both questions lies in
Jamaica's unique competitive structure and heritage.
To fully understand how an island with a population
of less than three million people can match and beat
a nation such as the United States, with far greater

economic resources and a population one hundred times larger, you have to see how this great sporting tradition has evolved.

In his book *Jamaican Athletics: A Model for 2012 and the World* Patrick Robinson* points out that runners from the island have benefited down the years not just from the competitions established, but a legacy of inspiration from successive generations, starting with Norman Manley. Manley's life was full of distinctions. He won a Rhodes scholarship, and was awarded a Military Medal for bravery in the First World War. He became a highly effective barrister operating within the British Commonwealth, and was one of the guiding lights in Jamaica getting its independence, ultimately serving as its Premier. But Manley might have chosen a different course – or track – for his life, given his talents as a sprinter. As a member of Jamaica College, he ran the 100 yards in 10.00 seconds (when the world record was 9.7 seconds) and the 220 yards in 23 seconds. The latter time would have earned him a place in the finals of both the 1908 and the 1912 Olympics. Clearly, here was a young man who could have been the first Jamaican to reach an Olympic podium. The testing ground for Manley, as for so many other great Jamaican athletes

---

* Patrick Robinson. *Jamaican Athletics: A Model for 2012 and the World*. BlackAmber, 2007

who would follow him, was a competition which emerged at the same time as he did, and which, in 2010, celebrated its centenary. Officially, it is the Boys and Girls High School Championships. But everyone who has ever been involved in this energising event knows it simply as Champs. When the event started, in 1910, there were six secondary schools and around 70 athletes taking part. Nowadays, this four-day event held at the National Stadium brings traffic in Kingston to a halt. More than 2,000 young athletes take part in front of capacity crowds of 30,000. Originally there were two or three development meetings before Champs. Nowadays the Jamaica Amateur Athletics Association's calendar lists around 27 preparatory and development meetings in the four months before the main event in March or April.

Many of these development meets, hosted by individual schools or colleges, take as long as 12 hours to complete, often requiring teams to travel from one end of the island to the other. For example, St Elizabeth's Technical High School, in rural Jamaica, regularly attracts 60 schools to take part in its Annual Invitational Meet. But if the numbers are bigger than when the first Champs took place, the passions are the same. Right from the start, Champs was always a big deal. So when Manley wanted to give full expression to his sprinting gifts, Champs was the place to do it. And he took full advantage of that opportunity, winning six events, a record that has never been equalled. His Champs record run of 10.00 seconds in the 100 metres was not broken until 1952 – a span that makes Bob Beamon's long jump record at the 1968 Mexico Olympics look shortlived …

The message to Jamaica's athletes was clear: it could be done – and it was being done. Just as Champs established a precious template for future runners, Manley's talent, style and achievement established a model for them to emulate. Since then, generations of great Jamaican sprinters have established their talents at Champs. Douglas Manley equalled the 100 yards record of his father, Norman. Then came Arthur Wint, the 6ft 4in medical student who became Jamaica's first Olympic gold medallist in taking the 400 metres title at the 1948 London Games, where his compatriot Herb McKenley took silver. Four years later, these two combined with George Rhoden – who had already taken the individual 400 metres title away from Wint, forcing McKenley to take another silver as both registered an Olympic record of 45.9 seconds – and Les Laing to beat the United States to the gold medal at the Helsinki Games. That performance has been celebrated within Jamaican athletics ever since, not least because of McKenley's inspired performance on the third leg, when his time of 44.6 seconds – on a cinder track – created the possibility of victory as it made up a deficit of more than 15 metres.

There were echoes of McKenley's run in the Olympic performance of Asafa Powell who, although he had finished a disappointed fifth in the 2008 100 metres final, recorded the world's fastest relay split of 8.58 in anchoring the Jamaican sprint relay team to victory. Is this how a heritage works? Maybe.

A photograph of the 100 yards final in 1964 shows Clifton Forbes (Technical), Michael Fray (St Andrew Technical) and the eventual winner, Lennox Miller (Kingston College), getting out of their blocks. Four years later these three athletes, along with Errol Stewart, would break the world record in the heats and semi-final of the Mexico Olympics before finishing fourth in the final, and Miller would win an individual 100 metres silver at those Games and a bronze four years later in Munich.

Robinson offers two other examples which, he believes, illustrate the innate Jamaican attitude of self-belief. Bert Cameron, who became Jamaica's first world champion when he took the 400 metres title in Helsinki in 1983, reached the semi-finals of the following year's Olympics in Los Angeles as a favourite for the gold. After 110 metres, however, he pulled a hamstring, hopping for 40 metres and losing at least 10 metres on his rivals. Most runners in that situation would have stopped. Eight years later, when Britain's Derek Redmond found himself in a similar situation, he decided to finish the course, limping home alone until he was supported over the final 70 metres by the substantial figure of his father, who had come down from the stands to assist his son. Cameron required no assistance. He resumed, and finished the race in fourth place in a time of 45.10 seconds, earning himself a place in a final which he now had no real chance of contesting.

The second example Robinson offers occurred during the 1996 Olympic 400 metres relay final, when at the final baton change Jamaica's Greg Haughton fell to the track. Instinctively, he executed a somersault – known in Jamaican dialect as 'kinpupalik' – and continued on his course, eventually bringing home a bronze medal. 'The role that Jamaica's success in global athletics has played in fostering national pride cannot be overestimated,' adds Robinson. 'The current crop of Jamaican athletes, including Asafa Powell, Veronica Campbell-Brown and Usain Bolt had Merlene Ottey, Juliet Cuthbert and Grace Jackson to emulate; those three had Don Quarrie and Bertland Cameron, who had Lennox Miller, who had Dennis Johnson. Of course, every athlete after 1952 had the great relay quartet of Arthur Wint, Herb McKenley, George Rhoden and Les Laing, and those four would have been inspired by Norman Manley ...'

Robinson goes on to quote Edward Seaga, a former Prime Minister of Jamaica and a sociologist, who contends that the lack of space and resources in which inner-city children live has produced 'a determination to aggressively and competitively overcome the odds of scarcity with challenging responses.' Robinson asserts that competitiveness, or assertiveness, is a key component of the Jamaican persona. 'Indeed,' he adds, 'there are some legendary stories of Jamaicans abroad standing up for themselves and others against brute force and injustice. It is well known that in London in the 1960s Jamaicans had such a reputation for defending themselves against racist skinheads that many persons from other Caribbean countries and even from Africa indemnified themselves as Jamaicans in order to forestall such attacks. This then – a rich athletic history and tradition, supported by the assertiveness, the combativeness, the self-belief and resilience that are native to the Jamaican persona – is the first explanation of Jamaica's success,' Robinson writes.

There's something about Jamaicans and running fast. Not only has Jamaica provided world-class sprinters down the years, to the point where they now dominate world sprinting in both male and female events, but many of the world's finest sprinters who have not competed for Jamaica have been Jamaican either by birth or descent, including Olympic 100 metres champions Donovan Bailey (Canada) and Linford Christie (GB), world champion Ato Boldon (Trinidad), world 400 metres champion Sanya

Richards (US), double 2004 Olympic champion Kelly Holmes (GB) and former world 100 metres hurdles champion and record-holder Colin Jackson (GB).

The innate sprinting ability of so many Jamaicans is something which Robinson acknowledges has prompted speculation over genetic factors. 'It has long been claimed that black people of the West African diaspora (to which the vast majority of Jamaicans belong) are genetically predisposed to excellence in sports that call for explosive talent,' Robinson says. 'A Jamaican journalist, Patrick Cooper, in his book *The Black Superman*, advances the thesis that there is a scientific basis for the dominance of blacks of the West African diaspora in explosive sports such as athletics, basketball, baseball, football, American football, boxing and cricket. To his credit, Cooper anticipates the objection that his thesis feeds into the stereotype of blacks as people with brawn and no brains; he, therefore, takes care to highlight the many achievements of blacks in areas outside the field of sports, and identifies the social and political factors explaining their relative underachievement in those areas.'

Bolt himself has no difficulty in embracing this idea of African influence, and has credited the African influx and its strong genes for the Jamaican success, along with the warm climate and increasingly good coaching. Part of Bolt's athletic accomplishment may be down to an even more local accident of birth – over the years his home place of Trelawny has provided an above average number of outstanding sprinters, including Olympic and world champion Veronica Campbell-Brown, Olympians Michael Green and Michael Frater, and the infamous Ben Johnson, the naturalised Canadian who was stripped of the 1988 Olympic 100 metres title for doping. Some scientific research seems to indicate that it is socio-economic, rather than genetic factors which are key. But whatever the genetics, generations of young Jamaican athletes have been able to rely upon regular competition.

If Champs is the main structure which supports Jamaica's upcoming generation of athletes, it is underpinned by a similar structure for those below secondary school age, which also results in annual finals at the National Stadium.

There is a clear network of competition throughout Jamaica, linking schools, districts and parishes. But Champs is its crowning glory. Robinson quotes from a *L'Équipe* magazine article by Sophie Tutkovis* in which she describes the atmosphere of the final Saturday night of Champs: 'Twenty-five thousand people who rhythmically clap together to the same beat. Yeah man! Shouting and chanting the names of their favourite schools. Still clapping ten minutes

* *L'Équipe*, 14 May 2007

after the end of a race. On a warm, moonlit Saturday night in Kingston, this is the final act of … Jamaica's most famous athletic meet.' Tutkovis relates the reaction of a visiting French coach, Jacques Piasenta, who had previously insisted that nothing could top the annual meeting involving 3,000 French pupils organised by the Union Nationale du Sport Scolaire: 'Tonight, he is speechless. "I have been to seven consecutive Olympic Games, from Moscow straight through to Athens, and I have never experienced an atmosphere like this."'

For all the wealth of talent in Jamaica, and for all the energies devoted to maintaining a competitive structure for young athletes, the level of success achieved could not have been reached without another network – that of coaches.

Many of the coaches who have worked within Jamaican athletics in the last 30 years are graduates of the GC Foster College, a gift of the government of Cuba which was established in 1980. Whereas before, Jamaicans had to go abroad to become coaches or teachers in PE, now there was a home-based establishment offering a four-year Bachelor of Physical Education degree. The dynamic effect this had on Jamaica's athletics coaching was soon mirrored by a similar shift in terms of the athletes themselves. Historically, Jamaica's finest athletes had taken up college scholarships in the United States once they reached senior level. Three of the famed 1952 400 metres relay gold medallists had established this pattern – McKenley went to the University of Illinois, Rhoden to Morgan State University and Laing to the University of California. Twenty years later Don Quarrie, who would win the 1976 Olympic 200 metres title, attended the University of Southern California, from which he graduated with a degree in Business and Public Administration.

The establishment of athletics training venues at the University of Technology (UTech), and later, at the nearby University of West Indies in Kingston proved an important forerunner for at-home coaching. In his time as Director of Sports, from 1971–2006, former 100 yards world record holder Dennis Johnson helped produce numerous athletes of international standard. Kingston is now the base from which two of the leading Jamaican coaches of the moment operate. The first of them is Stephen Francis, whose Maximising Velocity and Power (MVP) club at UTech includes Asafa Powell, 2008 Olympic 100 metres, gold and silver medallists Shelly-Ann Fraser and Sherone Simpson, world 100 metres silver medallist Michael Frater and world 100 metres hurdles silver and bronze medallist Brigitte Foster-Hylton.

Then there is Glen Mills, who runs the High Performance Training Centre at UWI – and coaches, among others, an athlete called Usain Bolt. Robinson relates that some of the impetus for setting up home-grown coaching establishments stemmed from a sense of anger at the way in which coaches in the United States regarded those in Jamaica. He quotes a recollection by Francis from the 1998 World Junior Championships in France, where he was told by some US coaches: 'Coaching teenagers is nothing, just babysitting. They are growing so fast that it does not require astute coaching skills to get them to improve. When they stop growing is when the real coaching comes into play, at 19 for girls, age 20 or 21 for men. You people in Jamaica can't coach. All you do is keep the teenagers ready and interested until we, the real coaches, take over.' Francis reportedly decided to set up the MVP club at that moment. And such was his subsequent commitment to his task that he once sold his car to make ends meet as he struggled to keep all his talented Jamaican athletes operating on home soil.

Germaine Mason, the high jumper who won a silver medal for Britain at the last Olympics, but who is coached by Francis in Jamaica, has described his coach as being like a strict father to his group, getting them up to train at five in the morning and frowning on the idea of drinking and partying. Had the MVP club competed as a nation at the 2008 Beijing Games, it would have finished sixth in the medals table.

The perception in Jamaica was that home athletes

were being run into the ground by their US univer-sities within the hugely competitive NCAA system. Quite simply, Jamaican athletes suffered regularly from burnout. Bolt has acknowledged that staying at home gives Jamaican athletes a better environment in which to train than the often exhausting US college circuit. Jamaica's US Ambassador, Anthony Johnson, maintains his country's athletic success is down to hard work, and cites his own list of reasons for his country's increased success in sprinting, a list which included a long-term national development programme, dra-matic gains in literacy and formal schooling, and emi-gration and technology. Jamaica, he says, already had a system of local, regional and national track champion-ships. But in the space of the past 30 years, enrolment in high school had increased from around 10 per cent to 95 per cent. Simply, there are now more talented young athletes around. And while talented home run-ners have started to stay and learn at home, Johnson added that the internet had made it dramatically easier to gain and share coaching knowledge.

With knowledge has come continuity. In 2007 Jamaica had the fastest 100 metres runners in the world in two age groups and the world champion in a third. At the senior level, Powell was world record holder with 9.74 seconds. At junior level (under 19), Yohan Blake had a national junior record of 10.11 seconds, while at the youth level (under 18) Dexter

Lee was 100 metres gold medallist. Blake has since become a sub 10 second and sub 20 second 100 and 200 metres runner.

Jamaica could also boast the world youth champion at 200 metres in the form of Ramone McKenzie. Taking bronze behind McKenzie was fellow countryman Nickel Ashmeade, who also won silver in the 100 metres and went on to take 200 metres silver in the following year's World Junior Championships. Continuity was also implicit in the statistic established at the 2007 World Championships in Osaka, where more than 90 per cent of the Jamaican team consisted of athletes who had represented their parish at the National Championships.

Behind the athletes and the coaches, credit is due to the organisation which put in all the hard yards to ensure that nationwide competition continued to take place – the Jamaica Teachers' Association. Robinson compares the efforts of Francis and Mills to fellow Jamaicans who had helped secure the island's independence. 'It is not to indulge in hyperbolic comment to say that they are doing for athletics in Jamaica what Marcus Garvey, Norman Manley and Alexander Bustamante did for our political life years ago. For what they are doing, and doing successfully, is nothing less than liberating Jamaica's athletes from dependency on a foreign system.'

But Robinson warns that Jamaicans should not be

lulled into complacency by their success, and stresses that greater financial support from the government is required to ensure continuity: 'In Jamaica there is a saying that captures very neatly the contradictions, more apparent than real, between smallness and greatness,' Robinson concludes. 'We say a person is little but "tallawah". This means that a person is small but strong. In global athletics, Jamaica is little but "tallawah".'

Since making its debut in 1948 at the London Games, this nation of 2.75 million people has won seven golds, 21 silvers and 13 bronzes in athletics at the Olympics. Since Arthur Wint and Herb McKenley finished first and second respectively in the 400 metres at the 1948 London Games there has been a succession of outstanding performances from Jamaicans. Bolt and Powell turned down scholarship offers from American universities, preferring initially to take up the offer of training at the University of Technology (UTech) in Kingston, albeit that there was nothing there other than a grass track and a weights room without any air conditioning.

It is a measure of the influence of Champs that the athletes who brought Jamaica four men's and women's sprint titles at the Beijing Olympics were former Champs champions – Usain Bolt, Shelly-Ann Fraser and Veronica Campbell-Brown. A year later, as Bolt annexed the two world titles, Fraser beat another

Champs champ, Kerron Stewart, to the 100 metres title in Berlin. 'Champs is the real deal,' Bolt told Donald McRae* as he attended its 100th anniversary running. 'The competition is fierce and the tradition is deep. If you can do well at Champs you can do well anywhere,' he said, adding that his sponsor Puma supports the athletics programmes of seven different competing schools.

Bolt's friend Colin Jackson, Britain's former 110 metres hurdles world champion and record holder, commented: 'I've been to a few championships in my time. And you know, the Olympics, the Worlds and the Europeans are all pretty good. They're OK. But this is different. This is Champs. When you come here you see the real root of the sport. The Jamaican kids have such desire to compete. It's incredible. And the knowledge of the crowds is fantastic. Inside that stadium will be women in their mid-60s who will be able to discuss the form of all these school stars. It illustrates the knowledge and commitment you find at Champs. I go into stadiums in the UK and I can tell you that spectators won't even know the names of the major stars in our sport – never mind high-school runners. At Champs you get to understand how deeply ingrained track and field is in this nation. My parents are both Jamaican, and I was brought up

---

* Donald McRae in the *Guardian*, 1 April 2010

with Jamaican culture, but I still couldn't understand why they had this passion for the sport. It was only when I came to Champs that I finally understood. This is athletics in its purest state.'

Bolt told McRae that his success at Champs, where he set 200 and 400 metres records of 20.25 seconds and 45.35 seconds as a 16-year-old, stood him in good stead for the pressures of later competition, something from which his friend and rival Powell, whose small school only reached Champs once, was unable to benefit. 'It has been a problem for Asafa,' Bolt said. 'He only got to run once at Champs and so he didn't have the same experience of this atmosphere as me. After running so much at Champs I don't worry about anything. Asafa is different. I've said to him he shouldn't stress too much or worry about the crowd. I'm always telling him this.'

Powell said: 'I love Champs. But I went to a very small school, Charlemont High in St Catherine, in south-east Jamaica, and we didn't get to qualify for Champs. We only made it one year and I got disqualified that time. Usain was four years younger than me, but he was always a big deal at Champs. He made his name there. That helped him because, for us in Jamaica, after the Olympics and Worlds, Champs is the next big thing. Usain learnt quickly how to handle pressure. That's why he was so cool in Beijing and Berlin.'

Grace Jackson, the 200 metres silver medallist at the 1988 Olympic Games, told McRae: 'Champs prepares these young runners for big-time competition. Most of us come out of poverty and Champs is our first real opportunity. That's not to say that rich people don't run. But maybe poor people run just that little bit faster because we are striving. So that's why all these kids are trying so hard – they want to win for their school and to get a better future.' Her views were echoed by Juliet Campbell, a more recent Olympic sprinter. 'Sprinting, for me, was a tool. If you ran fast you made it to Champs. If you ran faster you got to university and the Olympics. Sprinting is pretty much a way out of poverty. That's how it was for me following Merlene Ottey and Grace Jackson. And that's how it is for most kids at Champs today.'

Jackson added that the new strategy of trying to keep home-grown talent at home had been very beneficial. 'We now have Usain training at the University of the West Indies, here in Kingston, and that's a real carrot for youngsters. And we have cooked the carrot a little more by bringing his coach, Glen Mills, to the campus. So we're giving all these top athletes at Champs a real incentive. They can stay here alongside Usain and Asafa. And let's not forget the women. In Beijing, Jamaica won 11 medals. Three went to the men and the rest were won by the women.' The 100 and 200 metres at the 2010 Champs were won by 17-year-old

Julian Forte, of Wolmer's High school. He laughed when McRae asked him if he could be compared to Bolt at the same age. 'No way,' he said. 'Bolt at 16 and 17 was really extraordinary. There is no comparison between him and me. That's why he and Powell are my idols. I've not met Bolt but I talk to Powell and he's very encouraging. They both appreciate what Champs means and that's why they support it so much.'

Bolt's name now adorns the long white wall at the National Stadium on which the names of great local athletes are written, a list that starts with Jamaica's first Olympic gold medallist, Arthur Wint, winner of the 400 metres at the 1948 London Games. It was at the 2003 Champs that Bolt was first spotted by his sponsor, Puma – as the company's chief executive, Jochen Zeitz, recalled. 'Our talent scout had told me all about this kid, Usain Bolt, and we were looking for a new opportunity to do something from the grassroots up,' he told McRae. 'It was obvious this was a special combination. Champs is grassroots sport at its best and Usain was just fantastic. Our first commitment was to Jamaican schools but, out of that partnership, we found a superstar. Of course the glamour and success gives him a new aura but I can tell you that Usain in 2003 was not so different to Usain now. He was the same charismatic joker. We'd love to find another Bolt along the way, but that's probably impossible. There is only one.'

3

Bolt in the Making

USAIN ST LEO BOLT WAS born on 21 August 1986, and his starting blocks in life were firm – he comes from a close, grounded, loving and religious family. Bolt's father, Wellesley, pursued his initially reluctant mother Jennifer – he was a Baptist, she was a Seventh Day Adventist – and they settled together running the local grocery store in the rural district of Sherwood Content, in the parish of Trelawny, which is on the north coast of Jamaica. Trelawny was named after the Cornishman, Sir William Trelawny, who was governor of the island from 1767 to 1772. The area, about an hour's drive from Montego Bay, is known for its sugar plantations, and nutritious, yellow yams. Usain – who has a sister, Sherine, and a younger brother, Sadeeki – was born two years after the couple met in 1984, and they married when he was 12. By all accounts, Bolt was a particularly playful child, spending much money and time on computer games. His mother said it helped to keep him calm.

Bolt's given names arrived from two members of the family – his mother's young nephew-in-law suggested his first name, and his mother's sister gave him his middle name.

As a child, Bolt played football, and lots of cricket in the streets of Trelawny. But he began to show his athletic prowess while attending Waldensia Primary and All-age School, running in the annual national primary schools' meeting for his parish. At 12, he was the fastest 100 metres runner in the school.

When he moved up to William Knibb Memorial High School – which had an impressive athletics tradition and had previously produced Olympic sprinters such as Michael Green – Bolt's main interest was still in cricket, where he was a fast bowler, but his coach noticed his general speed around the pitch and suggested he concentrate on track and field. Oddly, Bolt did not idolise local fast bowlers like Courtney Walsh and Michael Holding so much as Pakistan's Waqar Younis. But cricket was fading into the background, although he remained a keen follower of the game and still plays cricket on public parks when he is at home.

Under the coaching of Dwayne Barrett and Pablo McNeil, a former Olympic 100 metres sprinter, Bolt was encouraged to concentrate his energies on running. Such was Bolt's talent that Barrett would sometimes look twice at his stopwatch to see if there was something wrong with it. At the age of 12, Bolt ran 52 seconds flat for 400 metres on a grass track in Manchester, Jamaica. Barrett recalled that Usain's biggest problem at school was being too nice, and that he had to be reminded that athletics was about individual success when he worried about having to race his friend Jermaine Gonzales over 400 metres. Gonzales would later accompany Bolt to Kingston and subsequently set a national 400 metres record of 44.40 seconds. His fellow PE teacher, McNeil, has similar recollections. He sometimes refused to let the young Bolt see the stopwatch in case it gave him ideas above his station. McNeil had to work hard to keep his exuberant charge in line, particularly when he decided to start playing practical jokes. But he predicted that Bolt's huge stride would take him to world record performances within the space of five or six years. With that talent, McNeil recognised, came a pressure that was greater than any previous Jamaican athlete had experienced. It was going to be a trial all round. McNeil, who was unable to watch Bolt earning his Olympic titles on television because his eyesight had been affected by a stroke, nevertheless correctly forecast his former charge's achievement in the Beijing 100 metres final, saying that he could break 9.7 seconds.

Maintaining Bolt's concentration as a youngster tested McNeil to his limits. He recalled occasions when he had to retrieve Bolt from the nearby town of Falmouth after he had taken a taxi there 'to flirt with girls.' McNeil would take him back to school – and the practice track. But for all his charge's occasional waywardness, he was always happy with the effort produced once work began. Some of Bolt's escapades pushed his coach's patience to its limits. But luckily for the young runner, and the world of sport, these impulses were bounded within a national tradition that is unique and extraordinary. And Champs, naturally, was the big testing ground for Bolt, as for so many Jamaican athletes before him. From the age of 12, Bolt was able to distinguish himself within the framework of this apotheosis of junior competition – although he did not make an instant impression. 'I first saw Usain when he was 13 years old,' Asafa Powell's coach, Stephen Francis, told Anna Kessel.* 'A skinny, tall guy. But then he went to the final and didn't do much. I doubted whether he would make the transition. I figured he would be trying to go abroad. I figured he would be lost like so many others before him.'

Bolt won his first Champs medal in 2001, aged 14, when he took silver in the 200 metres with a time

---

* Anna Kessel in the *Observer*, 24 August 2008

of 22.04 seconds. A few months later, performing for Jamaica in his first CARIFTA Games, he was second in the 200 and 400 metres, running 21.81 seconds and a personal best of 48.28 seconds respectively. It was in 2001 also that he made his first appearance in a global event when he competed at the IAAF World Youth Championships in Debrecen, Hungary. Racing against opponents who were two or three years older than he was, he failed to reach the final of the 200 metres, but lowered his personal best 21.73 seconds. At the 2002 CARIFTA Games, held at Nassau in the Bahamas, Bolt set under-17 records in the 200 and 400 metres with 21.12 seconds and 47.33. And within months he had improved those marks by running 20.61 and 47.12 at the Central American and Caribbean Junior Championships. The times were heading in one direction. The talent was undeniable. And, that summer a wondrous conjunction of three elements offered the possibility of a special athletic performance: Kingston, Jamaica; the World Junior Championships; and Usain Bolt.

On the evening of 19 July, at the age of 15 years, 332 days, Bolt became the youngest male world junior champion after clocking a time of 20.61 seconds for the 200 metres. It was an exceptional result for an athlete who, though grown to his full height of 6ft 5in, was still a relative novice in the sport, and racing against opponents who were two or three years older. But it was the victory that was vital – a victory that ignited a national stadium packed with 30,000 supporters. Afterwards, Bolt said that the time could have been better had he not had a bad start, but that winning the gold medal in front of his own people was the only thing that mattered, and was something of which to be proud. Bolt's race was run 10 minutes after the women's final, where Jamaica's Anneisha McLaughlin ran a personal best of 22.94 seconds but was beaten by Britain's Vernicha James – who, ironically, had been born in Bolt's own home parish of Trelawny before emigrating to the United Kingdom. Bolt had watched Anneisha race, and thought she should have won. So he dedicated his race to her, as well as to himself and his country, before rounding off his championships by being part of the 4×100 and 4×400 relay teams who set national records in winning silver medals behind the United States.

Dave Martin, who reported the event for the Press Association and the International Association of Athletics Federations (IAAF), remembers vividly the noise that crowd made – and the impact the emerging sprinter made upon the world of athletics:

Covering the championships was a fantastic experience, but without a doubt the highlight was covering young Usain Bolt. When I first saw him I couldn't believe he was only 15 years old. He stood head and shoulders above all the other runners in the 200 metres. He was already 6ft 5in. It was truly amazing. He'd shown us in the heats and the qualifying rounds what a vast talent he was. He may have been the youngest in the field, but you could see that you were looking at a world-beater.

When it came to the final, what a night that was. I remember being in the press hotel before the race, and it was already Bolt-mania then. I was told by the hotel security to make sure I got onto the coach early and get into the stadium because the streets would be packed. And they were – they were jam-packed. There were buses, bicycles, people just walking in the streets, all dressed up in the yellow and green national colours. They were roaring 'Jamaica, Jamaica'.

In the stadium it was unbelievable. There were more than 25,000 there – there wasn't a spare seat to be had. People were crowding the gangways, anywhere there was a space. The wall of the stadium was 30-feet high, and people were climbing up it, trying to get in, and the police were standing there on ladders and knocking them back down. It was just a total sell-out to see Bolt run that night. To win it in 20.61 was not exactly bad for a lad of 15. You knew as you were watching him run that you were watching someone who was going to be special.

At the press conference he spoke quietly, but he

was very confident. You could tell he was really serious about his sport. Even then he said he wanted one
day to be the best in the world. He would have got to
where he is now a lot more quickly if he hadn't had
all the injuries. But in a way I think that helped him,
because although it slowed him down, he could well
have burnt out and been lost to the sport if he had
carried straight on.

When we got back to the press hotel that night
it was well after midnight, and we couldn't believe
what we had just witnessed. We knew we had seen
an athlete who had what it took to be a world-beater.

Later, Bolt revealed that he had been so nervous before
the race that he had put his spikes on the wrong feet,
and that he had subsequently found it easier to run
in front of foreign crowds where the expectancy and
pressure were not so intense. Also present at those
championships was the former world and Olympic
100 metres champion Donovan Bailey, who had been
brought up in Jamaica before moving to Canada.
After watching the 100 metres final, where Trinidad
and Tobago's pair of Darrel Brown and Marc Burns
had taken gold and silver respectively, with Brown
registering a championship record time of 10.09, Bailey announced: 'The future of track and field is here
in Kingston.' He was right. But not quite in the way
he expected to be.

This momentous victory on home soil had elevated Bolt to a different level. 'Suddenly he was a big star,' Francis told Kessel. 'He got a lot of encouragement from the federation who wanted him to stay in Jamaica. It was the opposite situation to Asafa who had no choice but to stay, Usain had everything possible done for him to keep him from going abroad.' Germaine Mason, the British high jumper and silver medallist in Beijing who switched nationality from Jamaica in 2006, has been friends with Bolt since their junior days. 'I remember him at the World Junior Championships,' Mason told Kessel. 'He had three medals clinking around his neck when anyone else was lucky just to have one. There he was walking along, joking with everybody, clink clink clink.'

There was already concern in Jamaica that Bolt might be tempted by one of the six offers he had already had to take up sports scholarships in the United States. This was the route which had traditionally been taken by many of his sprinting forbears from Jamaica and the Caribbean region, and in many cases it had resulted in the athlete concerned being run into the ground on the American collegiate circuit. The situation prompted Howard Hamilton, who held the office of Public Defender in Jamaica's government, to write to the Jamaican *Observer* urging the Jamaica Amateur Athletic Association to make sure Bolt's future on and off the track was safeguarded. 'It is the responsibility of the JAAA to ensure that this new-found treasure receives nurturing and protection,' Hamilton wrote. 'Usain Bolt is the most phenomenal sprinter ever produced by this island and history will judge them harshly if they fail.'

By this time, Bolt had a manager in Norman Peart, a former athlete whom he had met on the training track they had both worked on. Peart had gone down to meet Bolt at the track where he himself had once trained with the idea of getting him a scholarship to the United States, something so many of his athletic forbears had enjoyed. But colleges did not take athletes until they were at least 17 – which meant Bolt had to wait. While his big future remained a topic for anxious discussion – and Puma signed him up on an initial sponsorship deal – Bolt was still producing outstanding performances. In 2003 he won the 200 metres at the IAAF World Youth Championships in Sherbrooke, Canada, as well as earning another gold at the CARIFTA Games in Port of Spain, with a time of 20.43. Another 200 metres title soon followed – at the Pan American Junior Championships in Bridgetown, Barbados. This was also the year when Bolt left his lasting mark on Champs as he altered the record books in the under-19 age group, recording an easy 45.3 seconds in the 400 metres, a 0.87 improvement on the previous record, and 20.25 in the curved sprint, to lower the old mark by 0.57. It was the third fastest time in the world that year. And it prompted Peart into a discussion with Bolt's parents that would have a profound effect upon the young runner's life and career.

Peart told them there was little point in him continuing to run for his high school having run 20.25, as there remained no local opposition. Instead it was planned for him to move to Kingston, where he would start training at the University of Technology on what was described as a five-year plan leading to Beijing, after which he switched his training base to the UWI. Bolt also had support from the former Prime Minister, PJ Patterson, who had felt moved to take an active role in his switch to the capital. But transferring this gifted 16-year-old away from home, and McNeil, to the capital proved to be a mixed arrangement, as the youngster began to succumb to injuries and off-the-track distractions – partying and night clubs. He began to suffer criticism for his conduct; the switch in location was starting to look like a bad idea. 'I was a mama's boy, so I missed my mum a lot,' Bolt reflected later. 'He almost lost himself,' McNeil recalled. Bolt liked his fast food and his bright lights – and he was convinced natural talent would see him through on the track. Natural talent was still working pretty well for Bolt, however.

As world youth and world junior 200 metres champion he had the opportunity of trying for an unprecedented treble as he prepared for his first senior global event, the 2003 IAAF World Championships in Paris. Even if, as seemed highly likely, the gold medal eluded him, Bolt, who was due to turn 17 two days before the championships began, still had an opportunity of becoming the youngest ever medallist at the World Championships since they had started in Helsinki 20 years earlier. His victory in the Pan American Juniors, a month before the championships were due to get underway in the French capital, had been achieved in a time of 20.13 seconds, equalling Roy Martin's world junior record set in 1985. That was a faster time for the year than either Konstadinos Kederis, the world and Olympic champion, or Maurice Greene, the leading US sprinter, had managed.

It was also much faster than anything that Michael Johnson, the world record holder with 19.32 seconds, had ever managed at an equivalent age. The Texan's best 200 metres time as a teenager was 20.40. Bolt's stated ambition before Paris, however, was relatively conservative – he wanted to set a personal best, even if he didn't make the final. Any improvement on that personal best would have made him the first Jamaican to have sole hold of the world junior record since one of his idols, Don Quarrie, who had run 20.56 seconds, aged 19, on his way to winning the 1970 Commonwealth title in 1970. Six years later Quarrie was Olympic 200 metres champion, and had a statue erected in his honour in Kingston …

Bolt had met Michael Johnson, another of his running idols, after winning his World Youth title. Johnson said at the time that the world's media would have to be careful not to overload the rising talent with the pressure of expectation. Bolt should be allowed to develop over the next five years. There were numerous examples of teenage talents whose careers faded after outstanding beginnings. For example, Dwayne Evans was a 17-year-old high-school student from Phoenix when he took the Olympic 200 metres bronze medal behind Quarrie and Millard Hampton in Montreal in 1976, and he never came close to repeating that form again. But there was to be no 200 metres final, or personal best for Bolt in Paris. There was to be, in fact, no Paris at all for Bolt as the Jamaica Amateur Athletics Association took the controversial decision not to select him, even though he had beaten all the seniors in the 200 metres at the national trials for the World Championships. The JAAA cited Bolt's youth and inexperience, taking into account also the fact that his training schedule had been badly disrupted six weeks before the Games because he had conjunctivitis. Their announcement caused widespread dismay in Jamaica – and not least in the parish of Trelawny. Perhaps the selectors had taken note of Johnson's advice not to put too much pressure on the youngster too early ...

For all his disappointment at missing Paris, Bolt

– who won the IAAF Rising Star award for the second year in succession in 2003 – continued to excel himself on the track. As a newly established professional in 2004, receiving coaching from Fitz Coleman, he lowered the world junior 200 metres record of 20.13 seconds he shared with American Roy Martin as he became the first junior athlete to break 20 seconds, with a winning time of 19.93 seconds at the CARIFTA Games in Hamilton, Bermuda. A hamstring injury in May prevented him from defending his world junior title. But at 17, he was still looking like a genuine prospect for an Olympic medal at that summer's Athens Games. 'It would be nice to be Olympic 200 metres champion at my age, but I don't want to harp too much on that,' Bolt said. 'I just want to continue doing well on the track and the results will come my way.'*

Despite his best efforts, however, problems with his leg – stemming from a long-term back problem – prevented him from giving anything like full expression to his gifts at the Athens Olympics, where he was eliminated in the first round of the 200 metres. But Bolt still believed in his abilities, even though he had been unable to show them to best advantage in Greece, and was already looking ahead to the 2008 Games. After returning from Athens, he began with

---

* Agence France Presse, 21 April 2004

a new coach – Glen Mills, who had helped guide Kim Collins, of St Kitts and Nevis, to unexpected 100 metres victories at the 2002 Commonwealth Games in Manchester and at the World Championships for which Bolt had not been selected the following year. Mills's previous athletes included Raymond Stewart, who finished sixth in the 100 metres final at the 1984 Los Angeles Olympics, and the man to whom statues had been raised, after whom roads had been named, for whom songs had been composed – Don Quarrie. Bolt's partnership with Mills would produce riches even beyond the dreams of Quarrie – eventually. But before that could happen, several critical adjustments had to be made – not least to the Bolt work ethic.

By June 2005, Bolt was declaring himself ready to make a serious flourish at the World Championships due to be held two months later in Helsinki. After qualifying for the team with an easy 200 metres win at the Jamaican Championships in a time of 20.27 seconds, Bolt announced: 'I am on track for the World Championships. Everything is coming together. I am in great shape and I am hoping to do quite well there.' Acknowledging the disappointment of the previous year's Athens Olympics, Bolt insisted that his work ethic in training was much improved since his failure in Greece. 'I am working much harder now. I really want to make up for what happened in Athens,' Bolt said. 'Hopefully everything will fall into place.'* He backed up his optimism the following month by smashing Iván García's eight-year-old 200 metres championship record at the Central American and Caribbean Senior Championships in Nassau, Bahamas, recording 20.03 seconds, his fastest time since his world junior record of 19.93, despite effectively running the second half of the race on his own. He dipped under 20 seconds once again in the London Grand Prix at Crystal Palace, recording 19.99 seconds. But although he did manage to reach these World Championships, his luck in Helsinki was out. Having become the youngest Jamaican male to reach an IAAF World Championship sprint final – 10 days before his 19th birthday – he suffered an injury in the chill, rainy conditions which blighted so much of the championships, eventually trailing home last in a time which no one ever had expected from the Boy Wonder – 26.27 seconds. Once again, he had been frustrated.

There was a more literal jolt in store for the 19-year-old when he returned to Kingston. On 19 November he was involved in an accident in which his car was reportedly seriously damaged. According to local reports, Bolt was returning home just after midnight when his Honda Accord was in collision

---

* Agence France Presse, 29 June 2005

with another vehicle. Norman Peart, Bolt's manager, denied reports that Bolt was in a critical condition, saying he had suffered only 'a small scratch to his face'. Peart added: 'All is well and he is fine and will be in school on Monday and back in training.' Peart added that despite finishing eighth in Helsinki, Bolt has put his performance at the World Championships behind him and was now looking towards running at the following year's Commonwealth Games in Australia. Peart went on to say that Bolt, who had a personal best of 45.35 seconds in the 400 metres, would soon be running a couple of races in that event in order to prepare himself for the next two years. It was an idea which Bolt did not exactly embrace.

Meanwhile his ambitions of making his mark in the world of senior sprinting continued to be frustrated. In March 2006, another hamstring injury forced him to withdraw from the Melbourne Commonwealth Games, where his friend Powell, by now established as the fastest man in the world, finally took possession of a major, if not global, title. The latest setback kept Bolt off the track for two months. But it had a silver lining for him – when he returned he was given new training exercises to improve his flexibility and basic strength. And plans to move him up to the 400 metres were put on hold … The general opinion within Jamaica had begun to shift a little as Bolt's meteoric progress appeared to be over and he struggled to complete a full season of running. The 19-year-old, for all his brilliance at the World Juniors in Kingston, was perceived as being in danger of becoming an athlete who might not deliver on all his huge promise, having failed to progress from the first round in Athens, and then fading to last place in the following year's World Championship 200 metres final in Helsinki despite clocking 19.99 seconds in the build-up to the event, citing another hamstring injury on his return. Peart responded by pointing out that Bolt was now on a special fitness regime designed to keep his back loose and supple and to help his general flexibility. The idea of switching seriously to one-lap running was dropped, as Bolt was encouraged to re-emphasise his potential over 200. When a long-awaited move to the Europe circuit arrived, the new re-emphasis on 200 metres sprinting – and the new approach to training – appeared to have paid off.

On May 30, Bolt indicated his refocused state by winning the 200 metres in Ostrava in 20.28 seconds, thus breaking the meeting record of 20.30 seconds set by Justin Gatlin in the year he won the Olympic 100 metres title. He said he was now upbeat about taking on Wallace Spearmon, the American world silver medallist from 2005 who had beaten him in London the previous year. And intriguingly, Bolt was also keeping the idea of the 400 metres in play.

A month later, Bolt had achieved the target he

might have managed in Ostrava but for bad weather – another sub 20-second 200. His time of 19.88 seconds, however, was only enough to give him third place in the Lausanne meeting as two US rivals broke through their own personal barriers ahead of him. Tyson Gay was second in a best of 19.70 seconds, but the race went to newcomer Xavier Carter in 19.63 seconds, a time only Michael Johnson had ever bettered. If Bolt was on a more competitive path, it was becoming clear that the competition around him was also getting tougher.

Two months later, however, Bolt claimed his first major world medal at the IAAF World Athletics Final in Stuttgart, finishing third in 20.10 seconds. And before the year was out, he had another medal, this time silver, from the IAAF World Cup in Athens, where his time of 19.96 seconds was bettered only by Spearmon's 19.87. Going into 2007, Bolt's confidence was rising as his body seemed finally to be becoming resistant to the injuries which had undermined his progress – injuries which mainly stemmed from a serious back condition, scoliosis – a curvature of the spine. Coach Mills reported that his new charge was suffering from poor co-ordination, and that his scoliosis was affecting his hamstring. Which meant a regime that consisted of not working so hard. Mills cut down on Bolt's high-intensity workouts and put him instead on a training regimen that emphasised strength and flexibility, building up his core muscles to compensate for his problematic spine, honing Bolt's body and technique until he was ready to fully harness his gift. Although Bolt continued to compete, for the two years of 2006 and 2007, he didn't place first in any races. It wasn't until 2008 that Mills's training regimen came to fruition, and the world took note.

Looking back on those years, Bolt reflected before the recent IAAF Diamond League meeting in Shanghai: 'From 2004 to 2007 I was pretty much injured every year. Because of my back – I have really bad scoliosis. So for me I went through some rough times. I was wondering if I was really going to get to the level I wanted to run. But after joining up with Glen Mills we solved the problem, we really worked hard on exercises. I have to do a whole lot of work on my core and my abdominal muscles to make sure my back stays strong. As long as I keep doing that then I should stay away from injury. We don't try to push my body too much now.'

With increased confidence came an increased sense of which events he wanted to be running. For all of Mills's desire to make him a 200/400 runner, Bolt was set on something a little less strenuous – 100/200. And so the deal which was to reshape athletics was made. Mills told Bolt that he could have his wish of running a serious 100 metres – but only if he broke Don Quarrie's 36-year-old national 200 metres record at the Jamaican Championships. Bolt accepted the challenge, running 19.75 seconds – 0.11 seconds inside the enduring mark set by his old favourite. Mills kept up his side of the bargain, entering Bolt for the 100 metres at the 23rd Vardinoyiannia meeting in Rethymno, Crete. Bolt won in 10.03.

And liked the feeling.

At that summer's World Championships in Osaka, Bolt built his career up by another significant level as he claimed his first senior global medal, running the 200 metres in 19.91 seconds. It was enough to beat Spearmon – but not Gay, who won in a championship record of 19.76. There was a second silver in the sprint relay, where Bolt, Powell, Marvin Anderson and Nesta Carter lowered the Jamaican record to 37.89 seconds in finishing behind the Americans, who clocked 37.78. Although Bolt had won no major golds in 2007, Mills nevertheless felt satisfied that his technique had improved significantly. The signs for 2008 were promising.

4

The Accidental World Record Holder

BUT NO ONE REALISED how swiftly and dramatically those signs would be transformed into athletic reality.

If Beijing was where Usain Bolt burst like a storm into world renown, the lightning announcing that arrival had flickered and flared two months earlier in New York City – late on a Saturday night of lightning, thunder and rain. Organisers of the Reebok Grand Prix of 31 May, staged at the Icahn Stadium on Randall's Island, knew they had an intriguing race in the 100 metres, where Bolt, in what would be only his fifth serious run at the distance, was due to meet the reigning world 100 and 200 metres champion, home runner Tyson Gay. Gay's double in Osaka the previous summer had clearly established him as the world's pre-eminent sprinter. But he faced a Jamaican challenge at both distances in the form of Powell, who had lowered his own world record to 9.74 seconds in Rieti a month after his disappointment at the World Championships, and Bolt – who, just four weeks earlier, had surprised everyone, including his own coach, by winning the 100 metres at the Jamaica Invitational meeting in Kingston in 9.76 seconds, the second fastest time in history. Bolt's performance in the National Stadium caused an uproar of approbation, and he did a lap of honour in front of 12,000 spectators who gave him a standing ovation. At the 50 metres mark he had accelerated away from a field which included two Americans who would reach Olympic finals later that year, Spearmon and Darvis Patton. The following wind was 1.8 metres per second, just below the legal limit of 2.00 mps.

Bolt, whose personal best beforehand was the 10.03 seconds he had run in Crete the previous year, told reporters immediately after the race that he had not expected the time. 'I knew that I was coming here to do under 10 seconds as my training was going pretty well,' Bolt said. 'During the race, I really did not know I was going that fast. I was looking at 9.80 or 9.85.' Asked if he could break Powell's world record, he had responded: 'I don't know … the night was just right, everything was just perfect, so you never know, this might just be one good race, but I am hoping it's not. I am going back to the drawing board and try to perfect the race better than I did tonight.' Mills described the time to reporters as 'fantastic', adding: 'I expected him to run about 9.80 but what surprised me was that he appeared to have eased up in the last part. In training he was showing me that he was going to run a fast time. I had him at low 9.80s but I guess with the adrenaline and so forth ...'

Gay, who had won the 200 metres earlier in the evening, also had high praise for the home runner. 'That 100 metres was amazing,' he said. 'Bolt is very talented.' In New York City, Gay was about to learn more about Bolt's talent. The 100 metres, scheduled as the last event, was eventually run even later than scheduled. The start of the sell-out meeting had been delayed by an hour in an effort to ensure favourable weather, but then the programme was held up for a further 40 minutes because of a lightning storm which forced the organisers to clear the infield and left spectators – many hundreds of whom were flag-waving, expat Jamaicans – scrambling for cover. When the rain cleared, spectators resumed their seats, spilling over into standing room on the backstretch because of the weight of numbers. Although efforts were made to clear the track, it was still damp with wet patches. And there was one more delay before the 100 metres runners got underway, caused by a false start which, it later transpired, both Bolt and Gay welcomed.

Seventeen years earlier, the Icahn Stadium had

witnessed a world 100 metres record as US runner Leroy Burrell ran 9.90 seconds. Now the spectators who had braved the rain were about to be rewarded with another world record.

As in Kingston, the man in the white vest with the lanky 6ft 5in frame moved inexorably clear of the field halfway down the waterlogged track before flinging both arms out in triumph and crossing the line in 9.72 seconds – and then roaring on round the bend as if he was running his favourite distance. Gay, all in black in the lane to Bolt's right, finished with a stunned expression in 9.85 seconds. So the world 100 metres record had been set by an athlete who, on his own admission, did not start properly, slowed down before the finish and was not even supposed to be running the distance seriously.

What could Usain Bolt do when he got it all together?

Bolt went so far as to say he was 'pretty happy' with his achievement in New York City, particularly as the meeting had been delayed for almost two hours because of storms. But he became more animated on the subject of the impending Beijing Games. 'This world record doesn't mean a thing unless I get the Olympic gold medal,' he said. 'Tomorrow if someone comes and runs faster than me, I'm no longer the fastest man in the world. If you're the Olympic champion, then they have to wait four more years to get you again. I think the Olympics is the biggest thing, and I'll be doubling in the 100 and 200 now, definitely. I always say the 200 metres is my favourite race. That's not going to change,' Bolt told reporters after his run at the Icahn Stadium which had made him appear ominously capable of challenging Michael Johnson's monumental world 200 metres record of 19.32 seconds. Bolt was now delivering seriously on the huge promise he had shown in winning two golds and a silver in the World Junior Championships aged 15, breaking 20 seconds for the 200 metres two years later and taking world 200 metres silver the previous summer.

In the aftermath of his Kingston effort, Mills had maintained that his athlete was 'a quarter-mile runner', even if their bargain at the Jamaican National Championships meant that Bolt was not now set on the course of running 400 metres races in preparation for his 200 metres challenge at the Olympics. Mills had gone on record as saying that Bolt was 'never going to be a good starter' because of the difficulty of getting his tall body smoothly out of the blocks. That handicap, despite Bolt's post-race assessment of his run as '99 per cent perfect', was compounded by other bad habits. When he ran the 200 metres, he still slowed by looking over his shoulder – 'Nobody stopped me when I was younger,' he said. He had clearly failed to push to the line in his 9.76 run, and did not drive through either in New York. The fates had been with him. His poor start when the race got underway was annulled because another runner had false-started. The following wind would also have been over the legally permissible level of two metres per second. Second time round, Bolt got away a bit better, and the wind gauge read 1.7 metres per second, inside the sport's allowable limit for record purposes.

Gay, 5ft 11in, lamented that he had run the same rhythm as Bolt, but that his opponent's stride pattern was bigger. 'He was covering a lot more ground than I was,' he added. Bolt appeared set to have the kind of impact over two distances made by Cuba's Alberto Juantorena, similarly nicknamed White Lightning, who won the 400 and 800 metres at the 1976 Olympics. Two years later, China's former world and Olympic 110 metres hurdles champion Liu Xiang recalled, as he sat next to Bolt at a press conference in Shanghai, seeing him for the first time when he had run at the 2005 World Championships in Helsinki. 'It was cold,' Liu Xiang said with a smile. 'And you quit when you were entering the curve of the 200 metres. At that time I thought, Usain is quite a tall guy and I wondered whether he is fit for sprinting. Three years later in New York 2008, after competing in my race I watched you beat Tyson Gay to get the 100 metres world record – and you couldn't stop after you reached the finish line. I really felt that you were galloping instead of running. When you are running you look as if you are at ease, so I just wonder if you are from another planet because you are not like someone from this earth ...'

For Mills, the coach who had taken over responsibility for Bolt less than a year before that faltering Helsinki performance, New York represented an astonishing – and unplanned – marker of achievement on a journey that was leading towards Beijing. Bolt's achievement was marked by a $1.8 million bonus cheque from his sponsors, Digicel, and prompted Mills to reflect upon the 'journey' they had both made since autumn 2004, adding that although the two of them sometimes differed in what constituted hard work, they managed to ensure their objectives were always met. Bolt joked: 'I got a call from Asafa and he said, "You've made things rough on me now."' But for all his satisfaction with New York, the new world record holder made no pretence of his impatience to set about the supreme task of becoming Olympic champion. Mills recalled the deal the two men had made the previous year in order for Bolt to have his wish of experimenting over the 100 metres distance – which the athlete kept to by beating Don Quarrie's Jamaican 200 metres record. 'He has always had the passion to prove to me that he is a 100 metres runner,' Mills added. He revealed that the plan had been to work on Bolt's speed in the early part of the season and then switch to improving the 200 metres in time for the Olympics. Clearly, The Plan, part 1, had worked well.

The goal, however, remained gold at the Olympics. And while Mills admitted that Bolt would compete in the 100 and 200 metres at the National Championships, he did not confirm the runner's assertion in New York that he would definitely double up at the Beijing Games. Games within Games were being played. But one thing was not in doubt. 'In terms of ability, Usain has the most of any athlete I have ever coached and probably have ever seen,' said Mills. Praise could hardly come any higher. Bolt's prospects of prospering in both sprints became even brighter on 14 July, when, at the Tsiklitiria meeting in Athens, he lowered his national record to 19.67 seconds, the fastest ever by a Central American and Caribbean athlete and the fifth fastest in history. Bolt's dominance in the 200 metres was expected, but he demonstrated it without faltering for a moment, entering the final straight with perhaps a two metres margin and finishing with an advantage of about ten. 'I am very satisfied with my performance. The crowd helped me a lot. I feel sure I will be very strong at the Olympic Games,' Bolt said. Although he still held back – or was being held back – from committing himself to both events, Bolt's prospects of becoming the first man to complete the Olympic 100/200 metres double since Carl Lewis in 1984 were appearing increasingly healthy.

In the space of a few months, the checks and balances between the world's three finest sprinters – Bolt, Powell and Gay – had shifted more than once. Judging by his bewildered comments in the aftermath of his New York defeat, on an evening when flaring lightning had announced a human bolt, Gay had been psychologically affected by the Jamaican's prowess. Physically, and metaphorically, Bolt had been on the American's shoulder the previous summer. Now he had signalled and manoeuvred … Bolt's compatriot Powell had been struggling with a groin injury, having made a belated entrance to the season's competition after injuring his right shoulder while lifting weights in Kingston in early April, a problem which required surgery in Miami. While he was recovering, Bolt made his big leap forward in the 100 metres. And upon his return to action he tweaked his right groin in July at the Golden Gala meeting in Rome. The man who spoke as quietly as Bolt, but with less confidence, was also struggling to dispel the idea that he was an athlete unable to rise to the big occasion. Powell's mediocre run at the previous year's World Championships, two weeks before running another world record in a race that meant relatively little, had hardly been convincing. Powell's upbringing had been similar to Bolt's – not wealthy, but upright – as he grew

up the youngest of six boys born to Cislin and William Powell, pastors in the parish of St Catherine. But
the Powell family suffered profoundly when, in 2002,
Powell's brother Michael was shot dead in New York
City, and a year later his brother Vaun died of natural causes while playing football. 'It was so shocking,'
Powell reflected later. 'I almost felt like, Who's next?'
His oldest brother, Donovan, a former world-class
sprinter, told him, 'Keep running.'

Which he did, recording nine sub-10 second timings in 2004, but only finishing fifth in the Athens
Olympics. It was to be the first of a series of disap-
pointments at major championships. The following
year Powell was injured as Justin Gatlin, the American who had taken the Athens 100 metres title and
would subsequently be suspended for doping, added
a world gold in Helsinki. Despite winning his Commonwealth title early in 2006, Powell faltered again
at the following year's World Championships. His
coach, Francis, commented: 'We're trying to help
Asafa cope better with pressure. We've also tried to
adapt his training to deal with the second day of races
at major championships; major championships are
not about the fastest man, but about the best man after
four races in two days. That's a very different thing.
Asafa has always had trouble on the second day.'

Despite all the disruptions to his season, however, Powell remained a threat, as he proved with

the narrowest of wins against Bolt in Stockholm on 22 July. Gay, who had come within a hundredth of his personal best in New York, had made up ground on Bolt when he broke the US record with 9.77 seconds in the quarter-finals of the Olympic trials on 28 June at Eugene, Oregon, and recorded a wind-aided 9.68 the following day. But while running the turn in the 200-metres quarter-finals on 5 July, Gay went down with a hamstring strain. Aside from physical problems, he had also had to sort out the organisation of his coaching team. In the off-season he had to decide whether to retain former Olympic sprinter Jon Drummond, who had acted as 'consultant' to Gay since the spring of 2007, or to return to his long-time coach Lance Brauman, who had been released from prison in September after a one-year sentence for embezzlement, theft and mail fraud. The dilemma tested Gay's loyalty and his competitiveness, and in the end he spent the winter in Orlando with Brauman before moving to Arlington, Texas, on 2 April to train permanently with Drummond. 'It's lonely in Texas,' said Gay, after a spring workout. 'But it's all business here, and this is what I need.' The New York defeat had jolted him. 'That race made us work harder,' says Drummond. The injury in Eugene was a bigger hurdle. 'There's no such thing as a minor injury five weeks before the Olympic Games,' said the four-time Olympic medallist Ato Boldon. Six days after the injury Gay went ahead with plans to move his training base to Germany, and 11 days after the strain he jogged lightly for the first time. 'It feels better, but I still have tightness in the hamstring,' he said that night. 'That works on a sprinter's nerves.' He was making the right noises in the run-up to the Olympics, but it was a critical hitch at a critical time. Bolt gave Mills much of the credit for developing his talent, although, as he admitted himself, his progress was partially dependent on taking a more serious attitude to athletics after years of – let's face it, under-standable – immaturity. 'I was partying too much, but now I am taking the sport seriously,' he said. 'It was time for me to change my ways and everything in my personality to accomplish my full potential. The World Junior Championships in 2002 opened my eyes to what I could do. I wanted to be like some of the guys who are my heroes in the sport – Herb McKenley, Don Quarrie, who is the finest bend run-ner I've ever seen, and Michael Johnson.'

Bolt's emulation of Johnson, however, was restricted very definitely to the 200 metres, although his coach continued to resist that judgement. 'I wouldn't say I am really lazy, but I don't like the 400 metres and I have never really wanted to make the necessary efforts for this distance in training,' Bolt said. Bolt's height had always made him stand out in the world of track and field. He towered over opponents in the manner of the 6ft 3in Juantorena – known as El Caballo (The Horse). In winning his Olympic double, the mighty Cuban bolstered the old notion that a good big 'un will always beat a good little 'un. Within four years, the slight figure of Sebastian Coe had unbolstered that assertion – but there was no question that Bolt's sheer size played a part in his success. 'It looked like his knees were going past my face,' Gay had said in the wake of the Icahn Stadium race. Ominously for his rivals in the build-up to Beijing, Mills believed Bolt could still improve significantly. 'He is not as strong as he should be,' he said. 'If he gets stronger, his stride frequency will improve and when we achieve that in perhaps the next two years, he is going to run even faster.' Just how much faster was something about which Bolt, sensibly, refused to speculate. But there was no such caution evident among some of the world's most famous sprinters. Maurice Greene, 100 metres champion at the Sydney Olympics, named Bolt as favourite to win the short sprint in Beijing. Canada's Donovan Bailey, the 100 metres winner at the 1996 Atlanta Olympics, said he could not only break the world 200 metres record of 19.32 second that Johnson set at the same Games, but could run '19 flat'.

Bailey added that in setting the world record 'it almost seemed like Usain had another turbo gear that he hadn't unleashed yet. Like it was a 120 metres race.' Even Johnson, Bolt's idol of idols, said he was ready to 'kiss his record goodbye' once the Jamaican started to operate over the longer sprint with the efficiency he had already demonstrated over 100 metres.

The accidental world record holder had it in his power to become an icon at the impending Beijing Games. A few days before he embarked upon his programme of competition, Bolt was pictured by a Reuters photographer sitting outside the lattice-worked Bird's Nest stadium, with the perspective allowing his outspread arms to take in its whole span, his Puma running spikes – with '100 metres Beijing' on their sides – gigantic in the foreground. As an image, it prefigured his performance beautifully. And the relaxation expressed in the photograph was evident as he went about his media business, hanging out in a 'Jamaican' bar at a Beijing shopping mall and being apparently surprised by the assertion that his coach had finally announced that he would be doubling up at the 100 and 200 metres. Asked whether achieving a 100/200 metres double would be a greater achievement in 2008 than it had been when Carl Lewis achieved it in 1984, Bolt said it would, adding: 'Just look at the quality of the opposition I would be lining up against in the 100 metres – the world champion and the former world record holder.' Bolt and his compatriot Powell both took some time off in Beijing to celebrate Jamaica's National Day – the 46th anniversary of the nation becoming independent of Britain. 'It means a lot to us and is a day to talk and reminisce together. I will still train but back home it is a day to do nothing and relax,' Bolt said. He and his fellow sprinters, male and female, were about to deliver a startling sequence of unofficial National Days to their proud nation …

5

Playtime for Bolt

THE PRESS CONFERENCE TO LAUNCH the second of the International Association of Athletics Federation's 2010 Diamond League meetings is underway, and Usain Bolt is sitting on a podium in the main hall of the Regal Shanghai East Asia Hotel, with a battery of TV, radio and other media reporters in front of him and black-suited Chinese officials either side of him. One by one, the officials stand to make their welcoming statements – which, one by one, are officially translated into English by a respectful interpreter. The contributions generate immediate applause from the Chinese-speaking parts of the assembly and belated contributions from English speakers including the semi-detached world and Olympic champion. Before sitting down, each official honours the applause by applauding the applauders themselves for a period of three or four seconds before deeming honour to have been sufficiently satisfied all round and resuming his seat. More than ever, Bolt looks like a freakishly tall boy – on this occasion, a freakishly tall boy forced to attend a speech day when the sun is shining outside and he'd rather, far rather, be out on the field playing. The fastest man in the world begins to look increasingly distracted until his attention settles on the black pad in front of him, and the pencil alongside it. He begins to sketch lines and doodle swirls, occasionally looking up like a guilty boy in class. There are no tellings-off. He resumes ...

Usain Bolt doesn't just like to play. He needs to play, and always has done. To the point where, when he was young, medical advice was taken as to whether he was hyperactive. Once the young Bolt got out of the house, however, he had the whole sunny parish in which to give full expression to his energy. It's well past 10 p.m. before Bolt is seated alongside the wounded local hero, Liu Xiang, for his post-race press conference at the 2010 Shanghai Diamond League meeting, an event that takes place in a room packed from wall to wall with media working to every kind of deadline. Bolt, who has won the 200 metres as he pleases in 19.79 seconds, has his own deadline. He is due to be outside the main entrance of his hotel to catch a 05.40 bus which will take him to the airport. Radio reporters are shouldering each other in an effort to get their microphones close to the overhead speaker – they look as if they are dangling from it. The interview process continues only fitfully as reporters ignore the procedure of waiting for microphones before they ask their questions. And as the two athletes wait patiently for each answer to be translated – either from Chinese into English or vice versa – before responding, what has already been a long night in the Shanghai stadium is becoming even longer.

Bolt's first question is almost an accusation – why has he not greeted his victory with the trademark arrow sign, which he had employed earlier in the week in Daegu when winning his 100 metres race? 'I did it so much in Korea, I guess I was just tired of doing it,' he admits with a weary grin. The Chinese media set about a prolonged inquisition of their former world and Olympic 110 metres hurdles champion, still patently haunted by the Achilles tendon injury which turned his defence of the title in front of a Bird's Nest full of desperately hopeful home spectators into such a sad and abortive spectacle. As the former world record holder deals with every gradation of the same question – How was your leg today? Was it the cold weather that stopped you winning tonight or was it your leg? Have the doctors given you an exact timetable for when your leg will be fully recovered? – Bolt's face took on a thoughtful look.

Was he contemplating the shape of a possible future? Or was he perhaps remembering the years when his own injuries had prevented him from showing the world what he could do? At the press conference held two days earlier, Liu Xiang had responded to the question of what he thought about Bolt with thoughtfulness and humour, concluding with his assessment that the Jamaican was 'not like someone from this earth,' adding: 'I saw you break your world records in Beijing. I hope you can stay away from injury and I will keep on watching you.' The response was a wide smile, a nod of thanks, and the offer of a handshake which was readily taken up. Here were two athletes who knew what it was like to carry the hopes of a nation on their shoulders.

Now the attention has turned to the Jamaican. He starts forward in his chair – boy looking out of the window after he realises he's just been asked a question by a teacher ...

Bolt's Jamaican teammate Shelly-Ann Fraser, who has matched his 100 metres achievements by winning Olympic and world titles herself, has already visited the Jamaica pavilion at Expo 2010, which has been hosted by Shanghai – a conjunction which has been celebrated in a song of questionable quality with the chorus: Better City, Better Life. So the question is this: will Bolt be visiting the Jamaica pavilion too? 05.40 bus. 'I think it's too late,' Bolt says. 'I'm leaving

early in the morning. I won't have enough time ...'
Finally, eventually, with the time approaching eleven,
the master of ceremonies announces the press conference has come to a close. 05.40 bus. And that there
will now be a presentation ceremony to both athletes
... For anyone who has followed athletics, it was possible to imagine many past performers responding in
a negative manner to this late extension of what was
already a late engagement. How many would have
reacted with graciousness? Well, Usain Bolt and Liu
Xiang both manage it. But as they take possession of
their trophies – framed impressions of their hand-
prints – before the official photograph is set up, Bolt
finds himself unable to retain possession, and the precious item falls to earth. None of the officials seems
to have noticed. But everyone facing Bolt has. And he
has. It is a potentially fractious end to a long evening,
but Bolt has suddenly turned the moment into com-
edy: features frozen, shoulders hunched, he shares
his awful secret with an audience already beginning
to rumble with mirth. And again, as he goes through
the slow motion pantomime of retrieving the fallen
trophy, there is laughter ...

When the wider world celebrates Usain Bolt, it
is for more than his prowess. Who would warm to
some growling figure, even if the figures on the digital clock did keep registering world record? What
the wider world has responded to in witnessing

Usain Bolt is the childlike delight he takes in run-ning, in playing, in everything, it seems, except train-ing ... The wider world – but not the whole world. Bolt's cavorting and dancing in the aftermath of his Olympic victories earned him censure from none other than the International Olympic Committee's president, Jacques Rogge. Rogge – an Olympic sail-ing veteran and former Belgian rugby union interna-tional – told agency reporters that he did not approve of Bolt's behaviour in the aftermath of the 100 and 200 metres finals. 'I have no problem with him doing a show,' Rogge said. 'I think he should show more respect for his competitors and shake hands, give a tap on the shoulder to the other ones immediately after the finish and not make gestures like the one he made in the 100 metres. I understand the joy. He might have interpreted that in another way, but the way it was perceived was "catch me if you can". You don't do that. But he'll learn. He's still a young man.'

Rogge went on to say that if Bolt could maintain his position he would leave a bigger mark on the sport than the great 1936 Olympic champion Jesse Owens. But it was the criticism, rather than the com-pliment, which made the headlines – a criticism that had been echoed by Trinidad and Tobago's four-times Olympian sprinter Ato Boldon, who commented that the 100 metres win was 'good TV, poor sportsman-ship.' Bolt's actions were widely defended, however.

Athletic Federations spoke out in his favour, and
Jamaican government minister Edmund Bartlett
maintained: 'We have to see it in the glory of their
moment and give it to them. We have to allow the
personality of youth to express itself.' Jamaica's Prime
Minister Bruce Golding responded more forcefully:
'It is pure red eye and "grudgefulness", he said. 'They
just can't come to terms with the fact that not only
has this little boy won the double sprint, but he did
it in world record time.' Rogge's objections, it can be
argued, stemmed from a cultural misunderstanding.
In producing his exuberant interpretations of the latest Jamaican dancehall moves he so loved – the 'nuh
linga', by one of his favourite artists, Elephant Man;
or, after the 200 metres, the 'gully creeper', apparently created by a friend of his named Ice – Bolt was
connecting with one of the mainsprings of his life.
The race he had just completed was a perfect expression of Jamaican culture – and here was another such
expression. 'It's a thing in Jamaica,' said Bolt. 'You
wouldn't really understand. I made it my celebration. My celebration to the world.' He added: 'I talked
to the other athletes and most are okay with it. I'm
just enjoying myself, that's pretty much it. I think it
makes the fans happy too because I'm showing my
personality. People enjoy watching me so I'll stay the
way I am.'

Meanwhile those who knew the way he was were

resisting the idea set forth of a disrespectful, even arrogant figure. 'Usain is very humble off the track,' said Germaine Mason, who won a high jump silver medal for Britain at the Beijing Olympics but has known Bolt for many years and trains back in Jamaica with Stephen Francis's group. 'He's not like what you see on the TV,' he said. 'I disagree with what Jacques Rogge said. When you win an Olympic medal that's the greatest thing ever, you don't just want to win and walk off the track, you want to entertain the crowd. You want to open up and express how you're feeling. His celebrations are a very good thing for the sport.'* Friends of Bolt described him as a young man who loves a party. After winning the 200 metres Bolt said he wished he was 'at the Quad', a nightclub in New Kingston where Jamaicans often see him out, bottle of Guinness in hand, celebrating his victories. 'It's like my second home.' Describing a nightclub as your 'second home' – it's not something that, say, Michael Johnson would ever have done. Even if it had been his second home. Which it definitely wouldn't have been.

Bolt's fellow countrymen had long expected him to run fast because they had seen him running fast for so long before he burst into world recognition. The process was similar in terms of his playful persona.

---

* Anna Kessel in the *Observer*, 24 August 2008

One of Bolt's predecessors as Olympic 100 metres champion, Britain's Linford Christie, once acknowledged that his involvement in athletics had kept him in a childlike, playful environment, and that, curiously, that environment allowed him to maintain his performance. But for Christie, that environment was bounded very definitely by the training track. In competition, he was fearsome, glaring down his lane at the starting blocks like an Easter Island statue, staring down any opponent, and especially any US opponent, who had the temerity to cross his path. The year after he won the 1992 Olympics, he added the world 100 metres title in Stuttgart – a race which, unlike the one in Barcelona, included the acknowledged master sprinter Carl Lewis and his US teammate Andre Cason. Cason was very small, very fast and very grumpy. Christie, comfortably over six foot, subsequently related how he had undermined the American's challenge before the race by deliberately stealing his lane on the practice track. So, there is playfulness and playfulness.

Bolt has never been 'edgy' with his fellow competitors. But, as he grew up, he frequently pushed things to the edge … Pablo McNeil, Bolt's long-suffering coach during the years before he moved to Kingston, recalled taking a group of athletes including Bolt to the island's capital in 2001 for Boys Championships and catching him sprinting away from the house of the late Prime Minister, Sir Alexander Bustamante, which was where the young runners were staying. In 2002, Bolt was due to run in the under-17 200 metres final of the trials for the CARIFTA Games, the annual junior competition for members of the Caribbean Community (CARICOM, formerly known as the Caribbean Free Trade Association), which were being held at GC Foster College in St Catherine. At the time when he should have been preparing for his race, he was spotted by a policeman leaving the college grounds in the back of a van. When Bolt returned, the policeman detained him – and sent for McNeil. The incident briefly created an outcry in Bolt's local community, where blame was attached to McNeil for involving the police.

Then there were the car crashes. Bolt's first crash, shortly after he had returned from the 2005 World Championships in Helsinki, left him with minor facial injuries. (And, according to his mother, Jennifer, it also left his Honda Accord a write-off.) A far more widely publicised prang occurred early in 2009 when he overturned his high-performance black BMW M3 into a ditch, leaving it crumpled, but got out unhurt, only to injure his foot – he was driving barefoot, naturally – by stepping onto a thorn bush. Such was Bolt's fame at this point that TV footage was taken of his car lying upside down in a field, and the right way up again with a dented, distorted roof.

Footage was also recorded of his own 'footage': as he left hospital with his mother at his side, white plasters were visible on the bottom of both feet, with one particularly large one stuck along the big toe on his right foot. Two days before the inaugural IAAF 2010 Diamond League meeting in Doha, Asafa Powell, one of the main attractions, attended a press function in the palm-fringed grounds of the Sheraton Doha Hotel. Bolt was not scheduled to be running until the next Diamond League meeting, but he might as well have been considering the number of questions put to Powell in which he featured. Powell, whose condo in Kingston adjoins that of his friend and rival, is a man who loves his cars – at the last count he had six – and he's not afraid to test them to their limits. But thus far, thankfully, Powell has not been involved in any spectacular road accidents. A question about Bolt's fitness for the road caused the quietly spoken sprinter's face to break into a smile. Two accidents now – would he be giving Bolt driving lessons anytime soon? 'He's got a car that drives itself now,' Powell said with a big grin. For the record, it's a 2010 Skyline GT-R.

Perhaps Bolt's automotive problem stems from the fact that he tends to treat his cars as if they are features in his beloved computer games. His mother once complained that, as a child, he had spent a lot of money on hand-held computer games. He's hardly alone in that. Yet playing those games is still a very important part of his life. Apart from the fact that he runs extraordinarily fast, Bolt is just a normal guy. He loves his music – his favourite performers are Elephant Man, Serani, Vytz, Assassin, Black Rhino and Beanie Man, although Mills prefers him not to listen to his iPod before a race because he believes it distracts him. Maybe that's why Bolt often seems to be singing to himself as he prepares for races. He loves his movies. He loves staying at home. And the normal guy also likes to lounge around for hours in his bedroom playing those video games with his younger brother. He loves his cricket. 'When I was young I didn't really think about anything other than sports,' Bolt said after his Olympic 200 metres victory. 'I played cricket and football before I turned to track and field. I still love my cricket, anyone who's aggressive, Chris Gayle, Matthew Hayden, definitely, Freddie Flintoff, because that's the way I played.' He loves his basketball – he's a fanatical supporter of the Boston Celtics. He loves his football – as a Manchester United supporter he fretted his way through their ultimately unsuccessful quest to retain their Premier League title in 2009–10. Towards the end of the previous season, when he was in Manchester to run in a 150 metres street race, he had visited the players at their training ground and offered Cristiano Ronaldo some tips on his sprinting technique. The pair of them were pictured pulling Bolt's trademark 'To The

World' bowman pose – pointing his left hand to the sky while cocking his right arm as if firing an arrow and it was hard to tell who was more thrilled to be with whom. Both so famous – it was like a duet by Bing Crosby and Frank Sinatra.

The Bolt sign has been taken up all over the world. It is used by NFL wide receivers. It is used by lumbering mascots in every sporting environment. In the teeming squares of Beijing's Olympic Park during the 2008 Games, it became the most popular photographic pose save for the one where you raise your hand to make it look as if you are holding the Olympic flame. Among the questions Bolt was asked at his press conference before the 2010 Shanghai Diamond League meeting was one seeking advice for others trying to establish their own trademark gestures. 'A pose is a part of who you are,' he said. 'It's a part of your personality. It's just whatever you want to do. You may see something you like. Anything is good as long as it's good for you.' In company with this innate playfulness is a revelling in the joy of his performance with those who watch, and particularly with fellow Jamaicans. This was the connection which inspired him to take the World Junior title in front of his own people against opponents three years older than himself. Video footage of that landmark victory shows the young Bolt running over to the main stand at the National Stadium amid a ferment of noise and flag-waving, and offering a deliberate, snappy salute. It was to be the first of many such flourishes on running tracks around the world which have diverted and delighted his supporters – and people who had just realised they were now among his supporters.

As he lined up to start his race of races, the Olympic 200 metres final where he planned to emulate the victory earned by his idol and compatriot Don Quarrie, Bolt shoved his face into the attending camera, bumping it on the lens and shouting 'Come and get me!' He retreated, then advanced again, singing 'Yeah, yeah, yeah …' This was a guy who was certainly not about to stop being different just because the President said he should. Less than a week after the Games finished in Beijing, Bolt won the Zurich Golden League 100 metres at the Letzigrund Stadium after treating the 26,000 home fans – who have long been to athletics as The Kop or the Stretford End's inhabitants have to football – to another vivid display before and after his run, bobbing and weaving like a boxer, and, of course, giving everyone the benefit of his exuberant trademark pose. 'I'm trying to take it easy,' Bolt reflected after completing his marathon hand-slapping circuit of the perimeter of the arena. 'I'm stuffy and not feeling too well. I'm coming down with a cold, so I wasn't able to think of a faster time. I concentrated on winning. My coach told me that I should make sure I ended the season healthy.'

Bolt's playfulness is genuine, but increasingly, deliberate. He says he does it as much for himself as others, in order to enjoy what he does. For without enjoyment, where, he asks, is the point? That said, Bolt has had to tailor his attitude in order to steer himself towards success on the track – which is, after all, far more enjoyable than failure ... Chris Turner, the IAAF Communications Department's Editorial Senior Manager, recalls a graphic illustration of how the man who loves to play indicated he had also fully embraced the need to be serious. It came when Bolt turned up for the 2007 IAAF World Championships in Osaka, where he ended up taking the 200 metres silver behind Tyson Gay. Turner believes that, although Bolt's progress had been undermined since his World Junior victory by a succession of injuries, there was a more profound reason for his failure to break through immediately. 'It was not so much injuries, it was the way he was looking at his life,' Turner said. 'He obviously had not trained as hard as he should in the past. When he got to Osaka, people were asking: "What's happened to all his chains and his jewellery?" He used to wear lots of it. He had all kinds of gold slinging around his neck. And this seemed like a visual sign that he had changed his attitude. It was as if a transformational thing had happened in his head.

'His coach, Glen Mills, was the one who had told

him what he could be if he did the training required. Usain also had support from his manager Norman Peart, whom he had known for years, and an agent in Ricky Simms – you couldn't find a more stable and reliable agent if you tried. I remember meeting Ricky regularly over the years before Usain started to succeed at senior level, and he would always tell me "Don't worry. Be patient. He'll do it.'"

After his post-Beijing victory at Zurich, Bolt offered an explanation for his flamboyant behaviour: 'I tried to let the crowd enjoy it,' he said. 'I wanted to make them feel like they were in Beijing. I tried to do as much as possible because they support us as athletes and I am very thankful to them for coming to support us.' Not for Bolt the stressed walk to the blocks. Not for Bolt the dissipation of energy on fretting and frowning, on worrying about every element of their race. When he gets to the blocks, the process, as he says, is simple: 'I just take a deep breath, go down, and let's go ...'

6

Bigger in Berlin

THE OLYMPIC STADIUM IN ROME has witnessed many outstanding athletics achievements down the years. It was there at the 1960 Games that West Germany's Armin Hary won the 100 metres title in a time of 10.2 seconds. In 1998, Hicham El Guerrouj set what still stands as the world 1500 metres record, finishing in 3 minutes 26.00 seconds, and the following year he returned to the Eternal City to break the old-fashioned mile record with 3.43.13. The performance that Tyson Gay offered over 100 metres there on the evening of 10 July 2009 took its place as one of Rome's all-time highlights. For this quietly spoken athlete from Lexington, Kentucky, the previous year had promised much – and delivered little. The 2007 world 100 and 200 metres champion was clearly shaken when Usain Bolt, the man whom he had beaten to the 200 metres title in Osaka the previous summer, raced away from him in New York at the end of May to set a 100 metres world record of 9.72 seconds. Tyson promptly set his sights on running 9.6, and his form at the US Olympic trials had offered evidence that that was not an empty ambition. In the quarter-finals he had broken Maurice Greene's nine-year-old 100 metres record with a time of 9.77 seconds, which made him the third fastest man in the world behind Bolt and Asafa Powell. In the final, he produced an astonishing, albeit illegally wind-assisted time of 9.68 seconds. But then, in the 200 metres, disaster struck when he injured his hamstring and he failed to earn an Olympic place in the longer sprint. Gay recovered in time for the Olympics, but travelled to Beijing with doubts in his mind, looking for a spot of good fortune. None arrived. He was unable to get beyond the semi-finals in the 100 metres, and his chances of earning at least one medal disappeared in the space of a few fumbling fractions of a second as Darvis Patton failed to pass the baton on to him as he prepared to run the anchor leg in the 4×100 metre heats. As the world went Bolt-bonkers, Gay returned home to puzzle over how to reclaim his pre-eminent position in world sprinting.

For Tyson, 2009 had begun, as had 2008, with high promise. He started his season by recording a personal best 400 metres of 45.57 seconds in May and then, in his first outing over 200 metres, he clocked a personal best of 19.58 seconds, the third fastest 200 metres time ever behind Bolt and Michael Johnson's world record-setting efforts. A time of 9.75 seconds at the US Championships, although it was again illegally wind-assisted for record purposes, nevertheless convinced him that, if he continued to improve his technique, he could beat Bolt's 100 metres world record of 9.69. It was with this mindset that Gay arrived in Rome to compete in the IAAF's Golden Gala meeting – and here, on a perfect evening, he enthralled the 35,000 spectators by improving Bolt's world-leading time of 9.86 by stopping the digital clock at 9.77 seconds. Writing for the IAAF website, Bob Ramsak described it thus:

Tyson Gay is back. With a sensational 9.77 runaway victory in the 100m tonight, the double world champion clearly demonstrated that Usain Bolt can expect serious company when the sprint wars begin at next month's World Championships in Berlin ... With a powerful surge beyond the midway point which he sustained through the finish, Gay easily beat back the challenge of former world record holder Asafa Powell, illustrating fully that the injuries which ultimately ruined his Olympic aspirations a year ago are a memory of the past.

In just his first 'competitive' 100m race of the

season, the 26-year-old American equalled his own national record from last year, underscoring his position as history's third fastest man.

'I feel that I'm improving,' said Gay, who clocked a wind-assisted 9.75 late last month in the first round of the US championships. On Thursday, Gay said that his health is back to 100 percent, and that he gives himself a 100 percent chance of retaining his two world titles. His 19.58 dash over the half lap in New York on 30 May and his performance tonight provide strong evidence to back up that confidence.*

But as Berlin loomed up, Gay's progress was undermined once again by injury – this time to his groin, something which was troubling him by the end of July when he won the 200 metres at the Aviva London Grand Prix, but in the less than spectacular time of 20.00 seconds, albeit that he had 'closed down' over the final 30 metres. A week earlier, Bolt had dismissed Gay's chances of beating him in the 100 metres, saying the American was 'more of a 200 metres runner'. 'Of course, I don't agree with that,' Gay said. 'He knows I'm the only one, or one of the only ones, close to either beating him or getting the record.' Like Tyson, Bolt had also started the season competing over 400 metres in order to improve his

---

* Bob Ramzak, www.iaaf.org, 10 July 2009

speed, winning two races and registering 45.54 seconds in Kingston. In late April Bolt suffered slight leg injuries in the second of his widely publicised car crashes, but swiftly recovered following minor surgery and was soon in England, coaching Cristiano Ronaldo on the finer points of staying on one's feet – and not a moment too soon – before recording the fastest time ever recorded for the 150 metres, 14.35 seconds, on a specially constructed track at the Manchester Great City Games. He then qualified for the 100 and 200 metres at the imminent World Championships by winning both at the national trials in 9.86 seconds and 20.25 seconds respectively, and indicated that his form was sharpening when he won the 200 metres at the Athletissima meeting in Lausanne on 7 July in 19.59 seconds. It was the fourth fastest time ever over the distance, just one-hundredth off Gay's best time, and it had been accomplished running into a 0.9 metres per second headwind and rain ...

The question being asked in the world of athletics was whether, having achieved his astonishing coup at the previous year's Beijing Games, Bolt could manage the even harder task of maintaining, or even improving, his standards. Having got to the top, could he stay there? The IAAF World Championships in Berlin would surely provide the answer to how he was coping with the pressure of being not just a supreme athlete, but a globally recognised figure who had already transcended his sport. The 100 metres final at the World Championships took place on Sunday, August 16 – exactly a year after the Olympic 100 metres final – but it began slightly later than its scheduled time of 21.35. The delay was caused by the fact that the crowd of 51,113 was still celebrating the silver medals secured by two home athletes – Jennifer Oeser in the heptathlon and Nadine Kleinert in the shot put. Indeed, when officials prevented the heptathlete medallists from completing their victory lap in order to allow the 100 metres final to get underway many of the spectators were not impressed, and the sprinters went to their marks against a background of booing … As he settled into his blocks, Gay knew he had done everything in his power to make himself a genuine contender for gold, having run under 10 seconds twice in the preliminary rounds to assure himself of an ideal spot to monitor his great rival. The American was in lane five on the blue Berlin track, with Bolt immediately to his left in lane four. From the moment the gun went, Gay put it all together. His reaction time was 0.146 seconds, fractionally faster than the Olympic champion's, and he moved smoothly through the phases of his race to cross the finishing line in 9.71 seconds, a massive improvement on his personal best of 9.77.

Gay was a distant second. Just like Frankie Fredericks of Namibia in the 1996 Olympic 200 metres final, when a massive personal best of 19.68 seconds left him in no-man's-land between the rest of the field and the vanishing figure of Michael Johnson, who lowered his world record to a scarcely credible 19.32 seconds. For Johnson 1996, read Bolt 2009. As in Beijing, the giant Jamaican had taken control of the race by the 30 metres mark. On this occasion, however, he kept pushing to the line – in the manner he had run his Olympic 200 metres race – and crossed it with the digital display showing a fantasy figure of 9.58 seconds. As Bolt embraced his friend and compatriot Powell, who had taken bronze in 9.84, the shock waves from his performance went through the stadium and the watching world. All the previous year's speculation about how fast he might have gone if he'd tried all the way had become reality as he took an astonishing 0.11 seconds off his previous mark. It was the biggest margin of improvement to the world 100 metres record since the hand-timed days. In the era of electronic timing, the nearest to it was the 0.05 seconds by which Maurice Greene had improved the record in running 9.79 seconds. 'I was definitely ready for the world record and I did it,' Bolt said. 'I didn't think I could run a tenth (of a second) faster than my world record, but for me, anything is possible. For me, it was all about going and winning, because I knew these guys were ready,' he said. 'Tyson was doing well all season. I think 9.5 is definitely a big thing. I'm proud of myself, because I'm the first man to do that. Through the season, I was just trying to get everything right,' Bolt added. 'Just trying to get back into shape. As you can see, I didn't run much in the 200 all season. I was taking it slow, trying to work my way up, take my time. But when it comes to competition, I'm always ready.'

Powell, for once, had run close to his potential in a big championship, although it was still some way away from his personal best of 9.72. 'I'm so excited about Usain's run tonight, it is great to be part of this,' said Powell. 'Usain showed us that it is possible. I'm disappointed to have lost the race, but I ran my fastest time,' said Gay, who had run the third swiftest race in history to improve his own national record. His time was just two hundredths of a second off his target – the 9.69 run by Bolt in Beijing. But he had been tangled up in blue. And now the target would have to be revised … For Gay, struggling with injury, the 200 metres was now a race too far. He withdrew from the championships, missing out on the 200 metres and the 4×100 metres relay, where his teammates contrived to repeat their performance of Beijing and drop the baton in the qualifying round. Reflecting on his year in an interview with *Spikes* magazine,* Gay revealed that his groin problem, which he had

---

* *Spikes* magazine, Spring, 2010

been carrying since going to Europe in early July, would normally have required surgery, but that he had resisted the pain in order to prepare for Berlin. It was eventually operated on in January 2010. Training sessions had to be curtailed and the weights room avoided for six weeks before the World Championships. Even so, he maintained, all four rounds of racing in the 100 metres event were agonising. 'I told my coach Jon Drummond that it was the most pain I had ever experienced,' Gay said. 'I was taking painkillers to try and numb the pain and get through the race. Jon couldn't believe the time I ran. "Knowing you were in pain, I really respect you." ... The way I ran that 100 metres in Berlin gives me a lot of heart and strength. Considering everything I went through, I think I have a lot more to look forward to.' Did that mean victories over Bolt? 'I guess I think I can beat him,' Tyson replied. 'I've never viewed anyone as unbeatable ... It isn't going to be easy, though.' Despite his withdrawal from the championships, Gay still went on to complete his season in 2009, and a month after the Berlin final, on 20 September, he won the 100 metres at the IAAF's Shanghai Golden Grand Prix in 9.69 seconds. Gay had finally caught up with Bolt – but only the Bolt of August 2008. The Bolt of August 2009 was still out of reach ...

Bolt had suggested in the aftermath of his 100 metres win that he would not be able to improve upon his 200 metres world record at the championships. The man whose record he had taken, Michael Johnson, agreed, opining that the new world 100 metres champion would be too tired from his efforts four days earlier. Other than the absence of Gay – although who knows whether that might not have spurred him to even greater effort – Bolt benefited from two other factors on the night. Firstly, the wind reading was only -0.3 metres per second, a more favourable headwind than the -0.9 mps in which he had finished his Olympic 200 metres final. Secondly, a false start by David Alerte meant Bolt had another opportunity to react to the gun after a slow initial timing of 0.345 seconds. Second time around his time was 0.133 seconds – the fastest reaction in the field. As in Beijing, Bolt was clear of the field as he entered the home straight, with the 2004 Olympic champion, Shawn Crawford of the United States, in silver position. Crawford was eventually caught by Panama's Alonso Edward and US team mate Wallace Spearmon. Bolt, now in a private race against the clock, stopped it at 19.20 before his time was rounded down to 19.19 seconds. Collective gasp followed collective gasp. Bolt had taken exactly the same margin off his world 200 metres record as he had his world 100 metres record – 0.11 seconds. And his winning margin of 0.62 seconds was by far the largest in World Championship history. Edward, who had begun 2009 with a personal best of 20.62 seconds, registered an Area record of 19.81 in second place and at 19 years old became the youngest ever world medallist in the men's 200 metres. His time was also a world age-19 best, breaking the 19.88 set by Bolt in 2006. A sign of the future? The future would tell ... Spearmon won his second successive world 200 metres bronze with a time of 19.85 – his third best ever clocking – while Crawford was run out of the medals in 19.89. Crawford commented: 'Just coming out there ... I felt like I was in a video game. That guy was moving – fast.'

Bolt, whose 200 metres win had come the day before his 23rd birthday, still had several targets in mind ... 'If Queen Elizabeth knighthooded me and I would get the title Sir Usain Bolt,' he told reporters. 'That sounds very nice.' Bolt was now the only athlete to hold Olympic and world 100 and 200 metres titles at the same time. Quite apart from the fact that he held the world records as well. He was also $100,000 richer, taking his total earnings from the championships to $320,000 from prize money and record bonuses. 'I never expected a world record tonight,' Bolt said. 'I was really tired but I told myself I just had to try to do my best. Now I *am* tired.' Tired he may have been, but he was far from being satisfied with his stupendous performance. 'I was too upright,' he said. 'It wasn't a good race but it was a fast one.' That was true enough. It was the first time in history that four men had dipped under 19.90 in the same race and also the first time in which five men had broken 20 seconds. 'I keep telling you guys, my main aim is to become a legend, that's what I'm working on,' he shrugged as he addressed the assembled media. 'It's a great feat for me to have broken my world record. I didn't know I was going to break it.'

Writing in the *Guardian*, Anna Kessel mentioned how reporters asked whether some would be suspicious of Bolt's latest exploits:

Bolt was direct in his answer. 'I keep telling everybody I'm clean; if they don't believe me there's nothing I can do. I don't know what else I can say to convince people I'm clean, only to just run and stay clean.'

Bolt said he was not upset by the speculation. 'I don't get offended because I know year after year people have run fast and then they have tested positive. I just continue running fast and one day people will stop asking that question.'

Spearmon, who took bronze, said: 'When we first started running in 2005 Michael Johnson had the record of 19.32 and everyone kept saying it couldn't be broken. Now Usain's done it and now the world believes. Somebody's going to break it again – maybe even him– it's just a matter of time.'

Asked if it was harder than his equally amazing

double in Beijing, Bolt said: 'Not mentally, physically it was harder because I wasn't in the best of
shape. The rounds took a lot out of me this time. I
just want to go home and sleep. It definitely means
a lot because I showed people that last year wasn't a
joke. I went through some problems this season but
I came out here and I showed the world with hard
work and dedication what is possible.'*

Bolt, as is his wont, had played to the crowd before
the race got underway, revealing a yellow Jamaican
T-shirt with the slogan '*Ich bin ein Berlino*'. This may
have been meant as a tribute to John F. Kennedy and
his famous announcement to the city 46 years earlier
that he was a 'Berliner'; or it may simply have been
honouring the bear mascot of the championships,
who went by the name of Berlino … Perhaps the
fatigue which Johnson had predicted did come into
play by the time of the sprint relay, where Jamaica
fell short of their previous year's world record time of
37.10 seconds, recording 37.31. It was still comfortable
enough to win gold, however, given that it was the second fastest time in history. By the time the 12th IAAF
World Championships had come to a close, Bolt had
taken three more giant strides towards the legendary
status that has long been awarded to the sprinter who

---

* Anna Kessel in the *Guardian*, 20 August 2009

achieved his finest hour in the same stadium at the Olympic Games of 1936 – Jesse Owens. Like Owens, Bolt produced not just one brilliant athletic moment in this giant stone stadium, but a series of detonations. When Owens collected his fourth gold medal of the Olympics as a member of the United States 4×100 metres relay team it was his twelfth event of the Games, including heats, in the space of seven days – he completed a unique sequence of achievement that still stands as an incomparable indicator of excellence. Owens' Olympic victories – in the 100 metres, 200 metres, long jump and sprint relay – were matched, in scope at least, by Carl Lewis in the 1984 Los Angeles Games. What gives Owens' achievement a deeper resonance, however, is the context. Unlike Lewis, who was feted on home soil, this 22-year-old son of Alabama sharecroppers and grandson of slaves was competing in a city where the racist ideology of the Nazi regime was building towards its full, awful intensity. And yet his natural charm and ability had the home crowd chanting his name along with those of their local heroes – a feat Bolt also managed in the same cacophonous space 73 years later. On the final day of the championships, the Associated Press reported, Bolt was honoured by the city of Berlin in receiving an original segment of the Berlin Wall – in fact, nearly three tons of it. Mayor Klaus Wowereit presented the sprinter with a small fragment of the wall, while the 12-foot high section was sent off directly to his training camp in Jamaica. The section of the wall, which divided communist East Berlin from West Berlin between 1961 and 1989, was decorated with a life-size painting of Bolt running on the blue track of the Olympic stadium and the words 'NEW WR' – new world record.

'I will never forget Berlin,' Bolt said at the ceremony. '*Ich bin ein Berlino*.' Wowereit said Bolt had shown that 'one can tear down walls that had been considered as insurmountable'.

7

How on Earth? …

SO HERE GOES USAIN BOLT, down onto his blocks. He breathes. He leaves. He wins. And look at the times … When Bolt steps up to do what he does, everything is simple. And yet the accompanying question, as with any startling accomplishment, is 'How?' Or to be more accurate: 'How on earth? …' Liu Xiang's recent jovial suggestion that this question was irrelevant, as Bolt clearly comes from another planet, will not satisfy. Statistics may tell us no more than lies, or damned lies. But the stats on Bolt's impact in his chosen events are irrefutable. Back in 1912, Donald Lippincott of the United States set a world record for the 100 metres of 10.6 seconds. These were the days when timings were only differentiated by tenths of a second. Nine years later the American sprinter who famously liked to throw himself through the finishing tape, the 1920 Olympic 100 metres champion Charlie Paddock, took a great leap forward in terms of his distance by bettering Lippincott's time by two-tenths of a second. Percy Williams of Canada clocked 10.3 in 1930, and the great Jesse Owens lowered the record to 10.2 in 1936, the year when he won the Olympic 100 metres title. That record stood for 20 years until another US sprinter, Willie Williams, lowered it to 10.1. But it was a European, West Germany's Armin Hary, who became the first man to record 10.00 seconds for the distance, something he achieved in 1960.

Although hand timing persisted for several years after the introduction of electronic timing in 1968, the record began to diminish in hundredths rather than tenths of a second thanks to the accuracy of the new photo-finish technology. In 1968 Jim Hines of the United States clocked 9.95 seconds, a mark that was not bettered until 1993, when fellow American Calvin Smith managed 9.93. The record now shows that 9.92 was the next officially recognised mark, set by Carl Lewis in 1988. Three years later, Lewis's US colleague Leroy Burrell lowered the record to 9.90. Lewis reclaimed it with a timing of 9.86 seconds a year later, but Burrell went one-hundredth of a second faster in 1994. Donovan Bailey of Canada ticked another hundredth off that time in winning the 1996 Olympic title. Maurice Greene took a chunk out of that in 1999, recording 9.79. Asafa Powell took another two-hundredths off that in 2005, and a further three-hundredths in 2007 as he recorded 9.74. Enter Bolt – with successive world records of 9.72 (2008), 9.69 (2008) and 9.58 (2009). So here is one measure of Bolt's achievement: to go from 9.86 to 9.72 took just under 17 years. Reducing the record by roughly the same amount again – 9.72 to 9.58 – took Bolt 15 months.

Ethan Siegel, a theoretical astrophysicist at Lewis & Clark College in the United States, has calculated that, judging by the incremental progression of the 100 metres world record over the past 100 years, Bolt appears to be operating at a level approximately 30 years ahead of his time. So just how does someone manage to do that? Part of the answer to that question as far as Bolt is concerned lies in his extraordinary physical proportions and the way in which he has brought them to bear in order to run very, very fast. Before Bolt claimed his first world 100 metres record on 31 May 2008, his coach, Glen Mills, had said Bolt was 'never going to be a good starter' because of the difficulty in getting his tall body smoothly out of the blocks. That handicap was compounded by other bad habits. When he ran the 200 metres, Bolt had a bad habit of slowing down because he would look over his shoulder, and that weakness translated to the shorter sprint, as he clearly failed to push to the line in recording his time of 9.76 seconds early in 2008.

His subsequent race in New York, where he secured his first world record with a 100 metres time of 9.72 seconds, also saw him fail to obtain the maximum from his momentum as he crossed the line with arms outstretched. After that defeat in the Icahn Stadium, Bolt's US rival Tyson Gay – a more normal-sized athlete at 5ft 11in – lamented that he had run the same rhythm as Bolt, but that his opponent's stride pattern was a lot bigger. 'He was covering a lot more ground than I was,' he added.

An analysis of Bolt's world record run showed he covered the distance in only 41.5 strides, whereas on average the world's best sprinters cover the distance in about 45 strides. Bolt might have completed that run in even fewer steps had Mills not compensated on what he saw was a natural tendency within his young charge to over-stride. The coach said he had put his emphasis on getting his man to run in as technically correct a fashion as possible, a process that took more than two seasons. Mills added that in 2007 they had worked specifically on correcting Bolt's running on the turn, making his movement more efficient as he went around the curve of the track. Mills was confident he could make his runner even better at 200 metres by stopping his tendency to lean inside and become unbalanced. By getting Bolt to lean forward, the 200 metres performance improved as the adjustment contributed to his developing a good first 100 metres. So that 100 metres speed, it seems, arrived as a by-product of an attempt to run the 200 metres efficiently. Ominously for any rivals, Mills said Bolt could still improve significantly despite the fact that he had broken the 100 metres world record, pointing out that his athlete was still not as strong as he could be. With added strength, Mills felt, would come an improved stride frequency – which would lead in turn to faster times over the next couple of years.

In the Olympic 100 metres final three months later, Bolt's stride count was virtually identical – 41.5, according to Mills. Powell, who could only manage fifth place, takes between 45 and 48 strides for the distance. After the final, Kim Collins, the 2003 world champion, maintained he had had to run two strides for every one of Bolt's ... Mills, a devotee of the 200 metres, surprisingly chose the first half of Bolt's 100 metres as his prize moment of the Games. 'We'd worked hard on my start,' explained Bolt. 'The first 20 metres has been my main problem. It takes time to get the technique right. I executed it right, so I guess that's why he's happy.' A year later at the Berlin World Championships, Bolt took 41 steps once again, with silver medallist Tyson Gay requiring 44. Bolt's height meant, inevitably, that he was a lot slower out of his blocks than shorter rivals. But once he got up to speed, that superior stride offered increasing advantage.

Bolt's performances have been sufficiently 'out

there' for some people to start proposing outlandish measures to allow his events to retain the element of competition. Simon Choppin, a sports engineer at Sheffield Hallam University, suggested soon after Bolt had lowered his world record to 9.58 seconds that in order to run faster than Bolt, fellow athletes may have to wear carbon-fibre springs on their feet and elaborate aerodynamic fairings. Or even have electrodes implanted in their muscles. 'What are sprinters to do when faced with an opponent like Usain Bolt?' Choppin asks. 'Sport statisticians say the extraordinary Jamaican's latest 100 metres world record came 20 years ahead of schedule.' So, Choppin asked, could technology give sprinters an edge over the Jamaican marvel? After toying with the idea of adopting carbon-fibre blades, or carbon-fibre ankle supports to guard against energy waste, Choppin allowed his technological fantasies to grow more abstruse as he looked further afield for possible means to gain an edge over Bolt. Skinsuits, he said, would offer sprinters less advantage than swimmers, but would still reduce drag, even if it only accounts for around eight per cent of their total expended energy. Or what about electrodes activating runner's muscles to ensure a perfect start?*

All very interesting; all very untenable. But the

---

* Simon Choppin in the *Guardian*, 19 August 2009

whole field of speculation is testament to Bolt's extraordinary impact upon his chosen field of endeavour. Before the Olympic 200 metres final, Michael Johnson – still world record holder at 19.32 seconds – predicted that although Bolt would be the one to break his record, he would not be doing it in that race as he did not feel he had sufficient speed endurance. It turned out that Johnson had underestimated Bolt's state of preparedness. 'Efficiency makes you fast' is the mantra of the man who caused athletics observers to sit bolt upright when he emerged in the early nineties running with the exaggerated uprightness of a guardsman. He appeared almost affronted. It looked almost as if he was moving along the track against his own will. And yet Johnson's will is iron strong. It was his will which allowed him to recover from the disappointment of being unable to perform properly at the 1992 Barcelona Olympics after suffering from food poisoning and to return and dominate the 200 and 400 metres distances to the point where, by the time he retired at the end of the decade, it seemed as if his performances were out of reach for a generation.

Until Bolt.

But the Jamaican, although he would no doubt agree with Johnson on the need to maximise his efficiency, is still a long way from being a model of control. Bolt's adaptation to the short sprint involves much that is unorthodox. Unlike the former world and Olympic champion Maurice Greene, he is not someone with the classic, muscular proportions to gain maximum advantage from the initial drive phase of the 100 metres. While squat, powerful runners like Greene drive out of the blocks, maintaining their low centre of gravity, Bolt, his long body bent over like a laptop, has the task of unfurling himself and getting his long legs into full forward operation. Before that happy state of affairs comes to pass, those legs perform some amazing contortions, on occasions pointing in directions very different from the conventional. And yet, during the Beijing 100 metres final, Bolt was already in touch with the leaders after 10 metres. And 10 metres further on, his giant stride was beginning to walk all over everyone. It is little wonder that his competitors sometimes have the air of children who have just been beaten by an adult. The whole thing appears rather unfair.

In competing at 100 metres, however, Bolt has to deal with a factor that is beyond his control. The recent history of this event has an unfortunate subtext, which is now usually available via footnotes. There you will find names which used to reside on the main list but which have since been removed. Such as Tim Montgomery, whose world record clocking of 9.78 seconds on 14 September 2002 in Paris was erased three years later when he was found guilty of doping abuse. Montgomery's demise will always be linked with that of his former girlfriend Marion Jones, with whom he had a son. Jones won five medals at the 2000 Olympics – three gold, including the 100 metres, and two bronze. All were stripped from her after she admitted in October 2007 that she had taken illegal drugs since before the 2000 Olympics and had subsequently lied to the press, sports agencies and two grand juries, a confession that led to her being sentenced to six months' imprisonment. The fall of this sporting couple followed the doping scandal centred in the Bay Area Laboratory Co-operative (BALCO) run in San Francisco by Victor Conte, a scandal which was set in motion through the anonymous provision to the United States Anti-Doping Agency (USADA) of a syringe containing the designer steroid THG (tetrahydrogestrinone), which Conte had helped to develop and which had been previously unknown and undetectable. That single act, which was followed up by USADA and the United States Attorney for Northern District of California, precipitated a mighty disturbance in the force of athletics. A large group of sporting performers, including baseball's Barry Bonds and British 100 metres record holder Dwain Chambers, were implicated in illegal doping. Chambers subsequently received a two-year ban from the sport. Having belatedly confirmed that it was he who had submitted the syringe – apparently after falling out with Conte over a financial matter – Jones's former coach Trevor Graham, who had won an Olympic silver medal for Jamaica in the 4×400 metres at the 1988 Games, was convicted of lying to federal authorities and banned for life by USADA for breaking anti-doping rules.

It was a dismal and truly sad web of deceit. But even the fall of Jones and Montgomery did not have the impact of the turn of events that took place after the 1988 Seoul Olympics 100 metres final, when Ben Johnson's stupendous winning performance in a world record of 9.79 seconds was swiftly undermined by a urine sample that showed up traces of a banned steroid – stanozolol. As Johnson returned in disgrace to his adopted country of Canada, the case reverberated across the world, eventually implicating a group of other athletes in the manner of the BALCO affair. It was not only Johnson's Olympic mark of 9.79 that was struck from the records. After he had admitted to steroid use between 1981 and 1988, the world record of 9.83 seconds he had set in winning the 1987 world title was also annulled. As was the mark of 9.77 seconds credited to the 2004 Olympic champion Justin Gatlin of the United States, which established him as joint world record holder with Asafa Powell. Gatlin's failed doping test in 2007 saw this time struck from the record. The sad truth about the 100 metres is that doubt goes with the territory. So it was hardly surprising that doubt should be raised by an athlete who was effectively a novice at the 100 metres and yet managed to break the world record at his fifth attempt, and to break it again in the Olympic final with apparent ease. Bolt has always been happy to address the obvious issue. 'When you break the world record, people start saying stuff but it doesn't matter to me,' he insisted to reporters immediately after his 9.72 seconds run in New York. 'When you know you're clean, it doesn't really bother you. I know I am working hard, so I have to assume they [other athletes] are working hard also. I see Asafa all the time, so I know he's good. He trains hard and works hard, so I know he's clean and is doing the hard work every day. We know there are athletes out there who work hard for what they want. I've been running good since I was young. The record is no surprise to me and other people. I just run clean and try to do my best. I try to lead by example.'

A couple of days after Bolt had run his first world 100 metres record, his coach insisted he would be willing to be tested at any time, adding that Bolt didn't even like to take vitamins. Within an hour of Bolt's 100 metres win in Beijing, Herb Elliott – the Jamaican team doctor and a member of the IAAF's anti-doping commission – insisted that anyone was free to come and inspect the testing system in Jamaica. Anna Kessel quoted Bolt in a report from Beijing:

'We've been tested a lot,' he said. 'I was tested four times before I even started running, urine and blood tests. I've been tested so many times now I've lost track. I have no problem with that, we work hard and we're clean and anytime they want to test us it's fine.'

It is an accusation that all Jamaicans involved in athletics have been defending against. Asafa Powell's coach, Stephen Francis, who first saw Bolt run as a 13-year-old at the Jamaican National Schools Championships dismissed the question. 'It's not explainable how they do what they do. It doesn't mean he's cheating, he's just using what he has. Usain ran 19.9 aged 17, when he was a skinny kid. Look at him now, 19.3 is not that surprising.'

'I can't stop people doubting,' said Francis. 'People always have a way of belittling or trying to explain things they can't understand by saying, "Yeah, Usain Bolt, he's cheating, he's not real." But in the world people come along who are exceptional. You have Einstein, you have Isaac Newton, you have Beethoven – you have Usain Bolt.'

What now for Bolt? Will anyone ever beat him? 'I've not yet figured out how he does it,' said Francis, 'but when I know, I'll try and find the boy to beat him. I don't think he's unbeatable but it's going to be a rare person who has the chance. A very rare person.'

As the rest of the world struggle to understand how anyone can perform such incredible athletic feats, Bolt is characteristically philosophical. 'I wouldn't say I'm a phenomenon,' he said, pausing for some time to think about it, 'just a great athlete.'*

Donovan Bailey, who had restored Canada's belief at the 1996 Olympics when he won the 100 metres title in a world record that didn't get revoked – 9.84 seconds – was unreservedly enthusiastic after Bolt's Olympic 100 metres win. 'Usain has brought excitement and belief back to the sport,' he told CBC TV viewers. 'When you look at him you see the most amazing natural talent, someone who has so much ability that he can surely win on his own terms.' But Carl Lewis, the winner of the Olympic titles in 1984 and – by default – 1988 was a little more ambivalent in his assessment of Bolt in particular and Jamaican sprinting in general. Lewis did not accuse Bolt of any misdeeds, but insisted that such leaps forward in performance merited the closest scrutiny. Lewis, who was cleared of positive tests for stimulants ahead of the 1988 Olympics, added that sprinting's recent past should automatically raise doubts over any extraordinary performance on the track. Asked early in

---

* Anna Kessel in the *Observer*, 24 August 2008

2010 by journalist Donald McRae* whether he felt the world now believed he was a natural force rather than a drug cheat, Bolt responded with a laugh. 'I think you've got to give them a couple more years. Jamaican people know we're clean but we have to convince the rest of the world. All I can do is continue running fast. But other guys have been cheating over the years – so I know where [the doubt] is coming from'. He can, however, now claim to be drug-tested more than any other athlete. 'They come when they feel like it,' he said of the testers. 'In January they bombarded me for two weeks – every single day they were at my house. And then I don't see them for one month. Then all of a sudden they're back again. So you just never know when they're coming.'

Bolt found himself being asked about the topic again in July 2009 when news broke that five Jamaican athletes had tested positive for a banned substance, even though the offences turned out to be relatively minor. Journalist Anna Kessel wrote: 'Usain Bolt last night expressed his shock at the news that five Jamaican athletes have tested positive for banned substances, calling it a backward step for the sport. The athletes have not been named, but at least two are said to belong to the same club as Bolt – the Racers Track Club – and are coached by Glen Mills,

---

* Donald McRae in the *Guardian*, 30 March 2010

although none are thought to be high profile. The triple world record holder, who last night won the 100 metres in 9.91 seconds in the London Grand Prix at Crystal Palace, said: "It's sad to know there is still drugs in the sport. It's sad for the sport because things were progressing well. This is a step backwards." Bolt acknowledged that the renewed speculation would bring his own performances into question: "They will question everybody again now, especially people from Jamaica. I get tested all the time and do my best ... It shows that when people get tested they get caught. I'm trying my best and Asafa is to show you can achieve things clean. People have to know you can't get away with it."*

The names of three of the athletes involved were soon in the public domain – Allodin Fothergill and Lansford Spence – both 400 metres runners who were in Jamaica's 4×400 metres relay squad at last year's Olympics – were reported to have tested positive for methylxanthine, a decongestant often found in cough medicine which was not explicitly listed on the World Anti-Doping Agency (WADA) prohibited list but fell within a category of stimulants banned by the agency. The Commonwealth Games 100 metres champion Sheri-Ann Brooks also received notification. Usain Bolt's training partner Yohan Blake,

---

* Anna Kessel in the *Guardian*, 24 July 2009

19, who finished second to him in the Crystal Palace 100 metres on the night when the news broke, was named by an official source, as was Marvin Anderson. Blake, Fothergill, Spence and Anderson received three-month bans and missed the IAAF's 2009 World Championships. Brooks later accepted a three-month ban from the IAAF for use of the same substance – methylxanthine.

On 14 May 2010, the Jamaica *Observer* reported that the World Anti-Doping Agency had approved the process which the newly established Jamaica Anti-doping Commission had followed in the case, where the initial decision to clear all the athletes because the substance was not on WADA's banned list was successfully challenged from within the commission itself on the grounds that it had a similar structure to a stimulant that was on the banned list. A further tremor went through Jamaican athletics in 2010 when Olympic and world 100 metres champion Shelly-Ann Fraser tested positive for what was believed to be another substance on the minor infractions list. For some, these cases will have confirmed dark fears. For others, they will have been seen as positive steps, establishing more rigorous anti-doping procedures within Jamaican athletics and showing up no more than a minor indiscretion or misjudgement. There was never any suggestion throughout the case that Bolt was involved. Chris

Turner, Editorial Senior Manager with the IAAF's communications department, has witnessed Bolt's development in the space of the last eight years and believes what he has seen militates against any idea that the sprinter is cheating.

'I remember doing the press conference with him in 2002,' Turner recalled, 'when he won the first of his IAAF Rising Star awards. He was in Monaco for the ceremony, along with the senior athletes of the year, Paula Radcliffe and Hicham El Guerrouj. Physically he was the same as he is now, the same tall, lanky athlete – he looked more like a high jumper, all legs. Since then, though, he has filled out – not so much physically as emotionally and mentally.

'There are always doubts about our sport – that's the nature of it. But when he came back to Monaco to pick up the senior award at the end of 2008, you could see for yourself. You thought, "This is the same guy. This is basically what we saw in Beijing – an enormous natural talent." He was just shining. It's fantastic when you have the chance to see the development of someone like that. You hear a lot about "Oh, he came out of nowhere." But that just wasn't the case.'

And having arrived, Bolt soon found that most of the speculation was turning towards the topic of where he might yet reach.

8

Searching for the Limits

AS USAIN BOLT PREPARED for the 2010 season, he could reflect upon two years of dramatic success which had established him in the world's sporting elite. He was preparing to launch his own clothing line with his kit sponsor, Puma, and had just announced a partnership with the Swiss watch designers, Hublot. Recently he had opened a new track at the University of West Indies made by the same manufacturers who had produced the track where he had set his latest world records in Berlin the previous summer. And yes, it was also blue. Bolt was also embarking on plans to open a sports bar in Kingston under his own name. This young Jamaican's achievements have already established him as one of the most celebrated athletes in the sport's history, placing him alongside others such as Emil Zátopek, Fanny Blankers-Koen, Carl Lewis, Sebastian Coe and Michael Johnson.

His appeal is patently obvious. One example – the worldwide TV viewing figure for the 2007 World Championship 100 metres final was 70 million. The figure for the 2009 World Championship 100 metres final, in which Bolt's involvement was eagerly anticipated, was more than 100 million. Bolt is everywhere, transcending his sport in the manner of a David Beckham. It is a fearsome responsibility to carry – but so far Bolt seems to make light of it.

Speaking in May 2010 on the eve of his run at the IAAF Diamond League meeting in Shanghai, Bolt reflected on how his life had altered since his feats of 2008. 'It's changed a lot,' he said. 'I've got a lot more media coverage now, a lot more sponsors. But personally I've tried to stay the same, to enjoy the sport and to keep working hard.' Asked to elaborate on his comments at the Berlin World Championships, where he had spoken about his wish to become a 'legend' in the sport, he responded: 'Over the years I've been watching track and field I've seen some legends in the sport. People like my fellow Jamaicans Don Quarrie and Herb McKenley, or Michael Johnson of the United States. For me I think it's a very strong thing to win championships and to continually stay on top of the world, so that's my aim. I've got two already and I want to really beat that. So I think it's getting there, but for me I don't think two seasons can do it. I think I have to keep doing this year after year, and it's going to take a lot of hard work, because these guys are going to be coming next season and the season after that.'

The prospect of defeat was not something he refused to entertain. But it seemed a distant prospect. 'I've said it before, I can be beaten,' he acknowledged. 'But I'm really working hard not to be. I can't say who will beat me – I don't know when I'll have a bad day. It might be somebody who is coming up, might be a youngster, or it might be one of the top athletes, you never know. I've been saying over the years I take everybody seriously. It definitely would make the sport more exciting, but the sport is exciting because there's a lot of guys coming through and there are also guys at the top who are great athletes, who train hard and try to get better all the time.'

Bolt, however, believes there are areas of his technique which still need to be improved. In the 100 metres, he believes his start, where his legs appear to go at strange angles before sorting themselves out, needs more work. At 200 metres, he thinks he needs to work harder on staying balanced around the curve. Bolt was also reminded in Shanghai that his split time during the Jamaican team's recent 4×100 metres victory at the Penn State Relays in the United States had been 8.79 seconds – from a rolling start in his position as the last runner. He was asked if he would be running under nine seconds any time soon as an individual 100 metres runner. The response was polite and immediate. 'That's something I don't think is humanly possible,' he said. Even for Bolt, it seems, there are limits. Asked by Donald McRae* how fast he might eventually run in the 100 metres, he replied: 'I think the record is going to end up at 9.4 something and then it's going to be stuck there a long time. It will be hard to break. But you never really know. Anything is possible.'

When Bolt looks beyond the span of his career, he doesn't see himself coaching others. He doesn't see himself, like Johnson, working for television and running his own high performance centre. Focusing. His take on life post-athletics is a lot simpler than that – although, it has to be said, vague. But then he is only 24. How many 24-year-olds can certainly chart their course ahead through life? Bolt has spoken in the past about his love of cricket, and his promise as a fast bowler, suggesting that if he had not turned out to be an even better runner, he would have devoted himself to a cricketing career. Recently he got the chance to bowl to his friend Chris Gayle, the West Indies captain, during a friendly match. Inevitably, the first ball he sent down was a bouncer, which he

---

* Donald McRae in the *Guardian*, 30 March 2010

followed up with the full eyeball treatment. A brief glimpse of what might have been, perhaps …

More recently still, Bolt has mentioned ambitions of becoming a football player in four years' time, and although it is hard to decide how serious such an ambition could be, the prospect of all that speed being deployed with any reasonable level of ball control is a heady one. There is, of course, a history of track and field athletes switching over to other sports to good advantage. Bob Hayes's performance in winning the 1964 Olympic 100 metres title with a time of 10.06 seconds on a cinder track in Tokyo mashed up by the previous day's race walk event is regarded by many experienced observers of the sport as being one of the greatest ever athletic accomplishments. Hayes, or to give him his full name, Robert Lee 'Bullet Bob' Hayes, went on to secure the US team sprint relay gold with a storming anchor leg before retiring from track and field and becoming equally successful in American football, where he played wide receiver in the National Football League for the Dallas Cowboys, winning a Super Bowl ring. The same path was followed to advantage by Renaldo Nehemiah, who dominated the world's high hurdling scene between 1978 and 1981, becoming the first man to run faster than 13 seconds, before switching to become an NFL wide receiver with the San Francisco 49ers.

But while there are many footballers who can run

fast, and who may have excelled as sprinters in their teens, there are relatively few established sprinters who have crossed over to the 11-a-side game with much success. One such was Darren Campbell, who established himself as one of Britain's best young sprinters, winning medals at the European and World Junior Championships before leaving the sport in 1993 to concentrate on football. Campbell embarked upon a respectable professional and semi-professional career with clubs including Plymouth Argyle and Weymouth before returning to athletics, where he went on to win the 1998 European 100 metres title, an Olympic 200 metres silver medal in 2000 and an Olympic gold medal in the 4×100 metres relay at the 2004 Athens Olympics. It seems unlikely, however, that Bolt will seriously consider switching his attentions to another field of sporting endeavour for anything other than his own amusement. His immediate course appears set, and it follows the line of an athletics track, whether curved or straight. Eventually, he says, he hopes to have his own business – a business where he can drop by a couple of times a week to check how things are going. 'I really don't want to work 9 to 5 – that's not good,' he adds with a boyish grin.

Life post-athletics might also mean he could drop into his favourite clubs in Kingston – the Quad, Fiction – and drink more than the Guinness which he says is all he allows himself these days. And practise his dance moves until they are razor sharp. And get onto the decks to pursue his hankering to become a proper DJ. It might also mean he could continue to look out for his mum, which he says has been one of the prime satisfactions of his material success thus far.

And he does like to see himself revelling a little in his past achievements.

But what records might the middle-aged Bolt be in a position to look back upon? Originally, it was only supposed to be the 200 metres, his favourite event, Quarrie's event, where he would excel. But Bolt's longstanding ability over the one-lap distance – aged 12, grass track, 52 seconds – has always left open the possibility that he might extend his career up the distances from 200 metres. Such has been the level of Bolt's achievement in the last two years that his coach, who had originally wanted him to run more 400s to build up his speed endurance for the 200, has had to accept that single-lap running – something Bolt patently dislikes – is not about to become a central part of his athlete's working life. Bolt offered another glimpse of his 400 metres potential at the start of the 2010 season when he clocked a meeting record of 45.86 seconds at the Camperdown Classic in Jamaica. Towards the end of May he again offered tantalising evidence of his adaptability by running the 300 metres at the Ostrava meeting in 30.97 seconds in what was his first attempt at the distance – exacerbating an Achilles tendon problem in so doing. That effort was just 0.12 seconds off Michael Johnson's world record. The American will have no great confidence in his record withstanding another effort, however, should Bolt decide to have another tilt at it. As for his estimable world record for the 400 metres – the 43.18 seconds he set in winning the 1999 world title in Seville – well, Johnson reckons its days are also numbered. Although eclipsing that mark will not be a simple matter for the Jamaican. 'That will be decided by the coach, and he has told me not to worry as if I am ever going to take up the 400 metres, he would design a brand-new training programme for me,' Bolt told reporters in Shanghai. 'Right now I am just concentrating on the next World Championships (in 2011) and Olympics (in 2012).'

Bolt was expansive to McRae on the subject of the 2012 Olympics in London, with its large Jamaican population: 'Oh man, I'm so excited,' Bolt said. 'I've been telling people it's going to be nerve-racking if you're not mentally prepared. If you're not ready for that, then don't go. Jamaicans are loud – very loud. They're not like other crowds who just sit around. And they don't just cheer after the race. They cheer before the race and then they go crazy. So that's why I'm looking forward to London. I'm a performer.

People love me and I love the crowd ...' If Bolt does manage to span from 100 to 400 metres, he will be the first man in history to do so. While Johnson made the 200 and 400 his own, he never excelled at the 100. And while Alberto Juantorena dominated the 400 and 800, the 200 metres was too short a distance for him. What may also come with some difficulty is excellence in another area of track and field altogether – the long jump. But Bolt remains enthusiastic about the prospect. 'I tell my coach I'd love to try the long jump before I retire,' he said in Berlin, where Mike Powell, the American whose world record of 8.91 metres is now nearly 20 years old, said that he believed Bolt – with his speed and giant limbs – could be the first man to jump further than nine metres. 'I could show him how, for a small fee!' Powell joked.

In the spring of 2009, before he blew the world's mind for a second time in Berlin, Bolt attended Champs, wearing his old school tie over a bright yellow T-shirt, responding to an endless stream of requests to 'do the pose.' 'It is good to make kids really want to get into the sport,' he said. Patently, here was a role model for all the thousands of youngsters seeking to follow in his lengthy footsteps. Meanwhile Lorna Thorne, Bolt's old teacher at William Knibb Memorial High School, is having to cope with so many children wanting to follow Bolt's example that the athletics coaching staff are having difficulty handling the demand.

It seems everybody wants to be Usain Bolt. But there is only one Usain Bolt.

9

Drawing Breath

ONE THING, SUPPOSEDLY, IS HARDER than getting to the top. And that is staying there. But having elevated himself to an astral plane in 2008, the star of athletics remained high in the firmament in 2009. Olympic titles. World records. World titles. More world records.

So what next?

What Bolt made clear, even before the start of 2010, was that, relatively speaking, this was going to be the year when he kicked back, eased off, slacked a little – call it what you will. Despite the demands of an expanded and imaginative new Grand Prix circuit, the IAAF Samsung Diamond League, this was going to be a season to provide a little breathing space after the superhuman exploits of the previous two. But he kicked off on 1 May by running the 200 metres in 19.56

seconds at the National Championships in Kingston. Which turned out to be the fastest 200 metres run in 2010 by almost two-tenths of a second. For Bolt's opponents, there was the problem writ large. Even when he was supposedly not eyeballs-out, he ran times that others could only imagine. Yet the Olympic and world champion was not to enjoy a smooth ride through 2010. Injury – and even defeat – awaited him ...

One of the big objectives of the IAAF's new competition in 2010 was to try and ensure that the big names of the sport met each other on a more regular basis. In order to be in the running for the prize due to the dominating force in each event – $40,000 and a nice diamond trophy – athletes were obliged to compete in at least seven of the 14 scheduled events, including the two culminating competitions in Zurich and Brussels, where double points were on offer. For Bolt, Tyson Gay and Asafa Powell, the three musketeers of the 100 metres event, there was a clear obligation to test themselves against each other, and Brussels, the climactic Diamond League event on 27 August, was announced as a definite venue for the three to race each other. The understanding was that there would be at least one other such occasion. And so, as far as the following public were concerned, the early form of all three men was put under scrutiny in an effort to discern who might end the year with the bragging rights, if not a global medal.

For Powell and Gay, 2010 was another throw of the dice; and if Bolt were not to be at full tilt, who knew how things might turn out? Bolt produced several other early flourishes after his impressive run in Kingston. He clocked 9.86 seconds for a 100 metres in Daegu, preparing to host the following year's IAAF World Championships, and earned another 200 metres victory at the Shanghai Diamond League meeting in 19.76. It was all looking good. But then his progress was checked by injury. Bolt took part in the Golden Spike meeting in Ostrava on 27 May with a view to making an impression upon the 300 metres record listings. Heavy rain militated against swift times, but Bolt pressed on to record a time of 30.97 seconds, the second fastest ever and the fastest ever recorded at sea level. But there was a price to pay, as he left the meeting with an Achilles tendon problem which forced him to scratch from his next scheduled appearance, at the New York Diamond League event, and which put him off the circuit for almost six weeks. Suddenly, Bolt's pre-eminence was open to doubt.

And so the first meeting involving the top trio took place at the IAAF Diamond League meeting in Gateshead on 10 July – the Aviva British Grand Prix. It was Powell against Gay. On the day before they took each other on at a track where Powell had equalled his then world 100 metres record of 9.77

seconds four years earlier, Gay had inevitably been asked to assess their relative merits. And of course those of their absent fellow musketeer. Interestingly, he named Powell rather than Bolt as the man who presented the greater threat – despite the fact that the world and Olympic champion, having had an MRI scan which indicated his Achilles injury had healed, had equalled Powell's season's legal best performance of 9.82 seconds at the previous evening's Diamond League meeting in Lausanne. Gay added that he had based his analysis on the fact that Powell, for once, had had an injury-free summer, while his Jamaican rival had struggled for fitness. 'Usain had a setback or two, but Asafa is healthy this year. He hasn't really had any setbacks, and that's the key. He's sharp, he's race-ready, and that's all you need in this game to stay on top.'

Powell had indeed impressed earlier in the year. Although neither of his main rivals had been present at the inaugural IAAF Samsung Diamond League meeting in Doha on 14 May, he had indicated his potential for the season by winning in a time of 9.81 seconds, with wind assistance of 2.3 metres per second, having run a wind-assisted 9.75 in his semi-final. The reigning Commonwealth champion had offered further compelling evidence that he remained a threat to the absent Bolt and Gay in the short sprint as he won at the Oslo Diamond League meeting on 4 June in 9.72 seconds. Although a following wind marginally over the legal allowable limit of two metres per second – frustratingly, it was 2.1 mps – meant his mark was not admissible for record purposes, it still matched his fastest ever time, which he ran after his disappointing Olympics.

And as he flexed his muscles and smiled for the crowd as they clapped and cheered him on his lap of honour, receiving the three 'hip hip' cheers reserved for Oslo high performers, Powell looked happy and relaxed. His rivals knew only too well that a happy and relaxed Powell was a dangerous Powell – as he had been on that unusually baking day in the northeast of England four years earlier. 'It's a good confidence boost,' Powell said. 'That's the best I've started in a season ever, so I'm feeling very comfortable and I'm just going to think about myself. Last year I had a lot of setbacks. I sprained my ankle and ran with a sprained ankle the whole season. This year the ankle is better, the shoulder is better, knees are better, I'm in a lot better shape than I've ever been.' But for all Powell's confidence, it was Gay who laid down a marker in Gateshead as he overhauled the fast-starting Jamaican to win in 9.94 seconds – an outstanding effort given the headwind of 1.7 metres per second. Although the taller runner established a lead at the halfway point, he was overhauled in the final 30 metres as Gay made his first 100 metres of the season memorable. Nevertheless the American, whose early season had been disrupted by a hamstring injury, held the back of his right leg after both his semi-final and final. 'I'm still rusty,' he said after the race. To which Powell, standing alongside him, responded with a grin: 'When Tyson says he's rusty, I know he's ready. I thought I was pushing through, but I started to ease it a bit too much, and Tyson came through.' Gay thus extended his 100 metres record against Powell to 9–7 in terms of victories after what was their first meeting over the distance since the previous year's Shanghai meeting, where the American had set his national record of 9.69. Six days later, at the Paris Diamond League meeting in St Denis, Powell found himself lining up alongside his fellow Jamaican – and once again he was outsprinted. Powell had to settle for a time of 9.91 seconds after Bolt had taken advantage of an unusually efficient start to win in 9.84 seconds.

So now the dynamics of 2010 were shifting again as Bolt and Gay drew notionally ahead. For a while it seemed that London's Diamond League meeting at Crystal Palace on 13 August might offer a rehearsal for the three-way contest set for Brussels. Bolt, however, chose not to race in the British capital, citing as part of the reason Britain's newly established tax law which had prompted other elite sportsmen such as Roger Federer to complain on the grounds that it sought to claim an unfair proportion of commercial earnings. And then came the announcement that all three sprinters would meet at Stockholm's Diamond League event on 6 August, the DN Galan meeting.

Bolt's arrival in the Swedish capital offered a vivid snapshot of the way in which he had managed to transcend, as well as to represent, his sport. There could hardly have been more fuss if Ronaldo or Beckham had come to town. And as the following report indicates, it was a state of affairs which chimed in particularly well with the affable Jamaican's psyche. Bolt, one felt, was easy with such fame, and Tyson Gay never could be.

The front cover of Sweden's *Sport Bladet* paper carries a picture of a sprinter arriving in Stockholm for his latest race. He's wearing a blue T-shirt and jeans, with a denim men's bag slung over his shoulder and a blue baseball cap set slightly back on his head.

Alongside his giant image are the words he uttered to the waiting world as he made his way through Arlanda airport: 'What's up? What's up? What's up? I'm here.'

Quiz question. Is this a) Usain Bolt or b) Tyson Gay? For those of you who guessed a) – well, yes, obviously. For those of you who guessed b) – I beg you, seek treatment. The way these two outstanding athletes engage with the wider public is as contrasting as their sprinting techniques. And I can't help feeling that the public dynamic works for Bolt in a way it doesn't for Gay. It is not simply that Gay, with a meek voice that puts you in mind of Michael Jackson, is an introvert and Bolt, affable and easy, is an extrovert.

Bolt, as he mentioned again this week at the press conference preceding the DN Galan Diamond League meeting in the Swedish capital, is a bit of a stay-at-home. He spends many hours at his house in Kingston playing PlayStation games either alone or with his younger brother. When he is on the athletics circuit, he heads not for the lobby, but the privacy of his room. But where Bolt differs so dramatically from Gay is the way he responds to the clamour of attention once he has left that room.

The press conference, in a cramped space within the Nordic Sea Hotel, was a perfect case in point. Gay preceded Bolt into the cockpit of jostling cameramen, photographers and reporters, and for a few moments his eyes seemed to widen with apprehension. 'I'm pumped up a little bit right now,' he said. Quietly. 'The reality is hitting.'

Asked how he liked running against Bolt, Gay responded: 'I don't know why you are all here, whether it's for me or for him. But this is the first time this year I've got this attention, and I'm loving it. Even giving autographs outside the hotel. It's great.' Well, he said he was loving it. But he didn't act like he was loving it. Having said he would not be following the proposed course of going to a separate table to answer further press enquiries – his name-tag awaited him along with three bottles of still water – he looked as if he wanted to employ one of his famous smooth starts and get the hell out. Bolt, naturally, revelled in the attention. Clearly he didn't want to be all day answering questions, but his responses were immediately engaging and interesting.

In sprinting terms, public appearances make Gay tighten up and bring a performance out of Bolt. Gay was asked a follow-up question by the event compere about his apparent surprise at being noticed: 'When you look in the mirror, do you see yourself as a star?' His reply was down-to-earth and instructive. 'This morning I saw that I needed a shave, so I got a shave,' he said. 'I guess I don't look at myself like that because my family don't treat me like that, if you know what I'm saying.

'Even though I've been here several times, every time I come back I'm still shocked to see that someone might want my autograph. It might sound naive, but I find it strange to think that people from another country should know me.'

As a follow up, both men were invited to ask each other a question. Bolt asked Gay about his daughter – who it transpires is already starting at the track.

Gay's question of Bolt was almost plaintive.

'I would like to know,' he said, 'how do you mentally prepare yourself, with all the excitement, before you go into a race?'

And the response said everything about the dynamic that has made Bolt into a figure who has transcended his sport.

'For me I kind of like it,' he said. 'I like the energy the crowd gives me, it helps me to relax, and it helps me to build up my motivation to get ready for the race.'

It doesn't mean that Bolt will win every race he runs. But it does mean that, whenever he goes to the line, he is able to access an enormous additional power. And that gives him another huge advantage along with his outrageous natural gifts.*

Bolt's relaxation was evident throughout that press conference as he responded to a range of questions that included the topic of retirement. The multiple world record holder said he planned to retire at the age of 30 after competing at the 2016 Olympics – assuming the event in Brazil went well for him. And he apparently ruled out the possibility that he would ever run a 400 metres world record. Initially, Bolt indicated that he was not thinking of extending

---

* Mike Rowbottom, insidethegames.biz, 5 August 2010

his Olympic career beyond the 2012 London Games. '2016?' he said. 'No. I don't think I will be. But it's Brazil, right? I think that will be my last Olympics. So I think I will retire at 30 if it's a good season.' Bolt also dismissed Michael Johnson's suggestion that he would be the one to beat the 400 metres world record of 43.18 seconds which Johnson set at the 1999 IAAF World Championships in Seville. 'I've been saying for a while that I don't want to run the 400 metres,' he insisted. 'I don't think I will ever do that, pretty much. Long jump is much easier.' He added that he hoped the recent changes in Britain's tax law which made it unadvantageous for high-earning performers such as himself to compete there regularly would be addressed and altered. 'I was supposed to do London, and you guys know about the situation with that,' he said. 'I had to get one more race in so we approached Stockholm. I definitely hope it's something they are looking at in the future, because there are a lot of Jamaican people in London, and I look forward to being able to race in front of them.'

The previous day this attempt at assembling the top trio of sprinters had once again fallen one element short as Powell had announced his withdrawal because of a back injury. Bolt sympathised. 'It's sad that Asafa's out because I think people were really looking forward to the three of us showing-down tomorrow,' Bolt said. 'I know what it feels like to be out. You train all year to compete, so it's really hard to have to sit and watch a race. I wish Asafa all the best so he can get fit and we can have the last race of the season. It's still going to be a quick time tomorrow because I am competing against Tyson and all the other guys so I know it's going to be business as usual. I like competing against Tyson and it's good for the sport. So I'm looking forward to it.'

Gay said he would probably need a personal best to beat Bolt in what would be only his second 100 metres of the season, and his third 100 metres meeting with Bolt following their race in New York two years earlier, and at the previous summer's IAAF World Championships. On both of which occasions Bolt had broken the world record. 'I think it will take a PB,' Gay said. 'If not, a fast time. I can't say 9.7 is not a fast time because it is, I can't say 9.8 isn't a fast time, because it is. But I know I am going to have to run my best to even be in the video, the camera shots ...'

Powell told the press conference that he was not sure when he would be back into action, although it seemed highly doubtful that he would be fit enough to race against Gay at the following week's London Diamond League meeting. 'I hurt my back three weeks ago and it's kind of weird because it's not getting better, so I am just hoping for the best,' he said. 'It's a problem in my lower back. I haven't had an injury like this before, and it hurts like hell! I've been doing a lot of work on it but I'm just taking it day by day. I made the decision not to run pretty much yesterday. I went back to the track and tried to do some things and see where I was at but things were still not coming together. I hope I will be fit enough to run in the Diamond League finals in Brussels, but I am taking things step by step, day by day. Hopefully I will be better by then.' And so the scene was set for Bolt v Gay III.

With its castellations, mullioned windows and keep-like tower, the Stockholm stadium – built to host the 1912 Olympics – has a uniquely venerable atmosphere. It's the closest you could get to watching athletics at Hogwarts. And on the night, events turned out magically for Tyson Gay, as the following report from Stockholm makes clear.

The world of athletics witnessed a highly unusual sight here tonight – that of Usain Bolt leaving the track as a non-winner. Two years after his last defeat – also on this track – the world and Olympic champion had to give best to the man who has got closest to his world records, Tyson Gay. After putting pressure on the lanky Jamaican with a characteristically swift start, the American was never headed, and Bolt, grimacing with the effort, was not able to make his habitual 70 metres surge, finishing instead in 9.97 seconds, the second slowest time he has ever registered in a final.

Gay, his face maniacal, sent an uproar of surprise through the packed 1912 stadium as he won in 9.84 seconds. It was a meeting record, earning him an automatic prize of a $10,000 diamond. But it is the precious victory he will prize above all else. On a sunny evening when Alice Cooper – playing in Stockholm this weekend – had said an earlier hello to a packed stadium on an open-top car circuit of the track – it was Gay who showed there was 'No More Mr Nice Guy'.

As Bolt, who appeared to have given up hope of beating his rival in the final few metres, made a neutral exit, the photographers on the track were seized by indecision over which athlete to capture. Characteristically there were no trademark poses or antics from Gay, who acknowledged his first victory over Bolt in three attempts with little more than a perfunctory raising of his arm. It was nevertheless a significant marker for Gay – and an indication, perhaps, that Bolt had not been bluffing when he had said earlier in the week that he had tended to slack in training this year. But if Bolt had failed in his objective of staying undefeated this season, he appeared to have achieved his other ambition of avoiding injury.

Gay had arrived with happy memories of Stockholm, having won here the previous year in a wind-assisted time of 9.79 in a race where former world record holder Asafa Powell had had to drop out of this race at late notice with a back injury. For Bolt, the vibe was less promising, as it was on this track two years ago that he had suffered his last defeat, headed to the 100 metres line by Powell, who finished 0.01 seconds ahead. There had been massive cheers for Bolt when he was introduced to the crowd, suspiciously many of whom at the finishing end were brandishing little Jamaican flags on sticks. Whoever was in Gay's camp had conspicuously failed to match this allocation with Stars and Stripes.

By the time the final got underway the sun had dipped below the rim of the venerable stadium, built for the 1912 Olympics. But if the sun was dipping, Gay's star was rising. 'Now I've got to keep it up,' Gay said. Bolt was phlegmatic in defeat. 'Just one of those days,' he said. 'I told you I'm not unbeatable. I did not train as hard as in past years, so I can't complain. And it was Tyson Gay. My congratulations to him. I'm not in my best shape and he is in great shape. I still have a relay in Zurich and the 100 metres in Brussels to finish the season. I simply wasn't ready enough for that clash.' Gay added: 'I'm happy with the victory, but still looking forward to when Usain and Asafa will be in 9.6 shape to race with them. My body worked well today. I was excited and motivated. My start was okay and I must admit I was surprised not to be seeing Usain in front after half of the race. But I knew he was not 100 per cent ready. Still, it feels good to be the winner. But I think I can run a lot faster.'*

Gay's prediction would soon be borne out. But he would not have Bolt there to encourage him. Within a week, the world record holder had declared his competitive interest in 2010 to be over, a decision he had reached in order to prevent his ongoing lower back problems from becoming unmanageable. Bolt's decision meant he would now miss the billed showdown between himself, Gay and Powell which had been scheduled for Brussels on 27 August. Bolt was also out of his scheduled relay run at the following week's Zurich Diamond League meeting. A Munich doctor who examined Bolt three days after his Stockholm defeat had found a problem with the Jamaican's lower back, which, if not treated, could have caused injury to his hamstring or calf muscles. Bolt's development as a senior athlete, of course, had been threatened by a lower back injury which he had learned to alleviate with the help of strengthening exercises for his core muscles. 'With a view to his future career, we believe further treatment to loosen his back, followed by a period of rest, will be in his best interests,' Ricky

---

* Mike Rowbottom, insidethegames.biz, 6 August 2010

Simms, the sprint star's agent, said in a statement. 'I am very disappointed to miss two of the top meetings on the circuit,' said Bolt, who added that he was targeting the following year's IAAF World Championships in Daegu, South Korea, and the London 2012 Olympics. 'But trust that it is better for me not to take any risks this year. 2011 and 2012 are very important championship years and I hope to be back fully fit and healthy.'

At the time, Bolt shared the fastest 100 metres time of the year with Powell – 9.82 seconds. He had, on his own admission, not been at the top of his form. But then this was a man, not a robot. Gay, meanwhile, was pursuing what he likes to call 'the numbers'. He was after a fast time – and within a week of his Stockholm flourish he had found it, in the unpromising surroundings of a damp, nay sodden, stadium in south London. After getting a start that was exceptional even by his exalted standards, Gay moved clear of the field to flash across the line in a time that sent a roar of disbelief through the stands – 9.78 seconds, 0.04 seconds faster than Bolt and Powell's joint best for the year. It was also a memorable run for Bolt's 20-year-old training partner Yohan Blake, who recorded a personal best of 9.89 seconds.

Gay, who felt his fragile groin area after the race, said: 'I wasn't expecting to go that fast in these conditions but I knew I was in good shape. I was hobbling a bit at the end – my groin is a little sore, but I'm sure it's okay. I think there's more to come.' Gay was right again – but he was not to run any faster. By the time that the Brussels showdown arrived, he had victories over both his Jamaican rivals to his credit. He was still in cracking form. He was also the last man standing, with Powell having followed Bolt's example of calling time on the season as a precaution ... In damp conditions similar to London, Gay duly won his third consecutive Samsung Diamond League 100 metres – and with it, an extra hunk of money and a trophy to take home – with another top quality performance, clocking 9.79 seconds. However, the presence of Bolt's fellow Jamaican Nesta Carter ensured that the American did not have much leeway as he headed the race over the opening 30 metres and finished with a personal best of 9.85 seconds. He would end the season level on 9.78 with Gay after running even more swiftly at the meeting in Rieti. Blake also underlined his massive potential by defying the elements to record another sub-10 performance – 9.91. The depth of Jamaica's sprinting talent was being underlined once again, but an American held sway – if only for the moment. 'It's great to be on top of the world,' said Gay. Humbly. But how long would it last?

While Gay enjoyed a feeling of satisfaction, albeit not one of unalloyed triumph, Bolt was carrying on with his alternative life as a global icon. At the end of

August, Puma, the German sports manufacturers who have backed Bolt since he was 16, announced that he had signed a new contract that was 'by far the largest ever given to a track and field athlete'. Although Puma did not reveal the value, marketing experts estimated the deal could be worth £10 million to Bolt over three years. Puma chairman and CEO Jochen Zeitz said of Bolt: 'He's an iconic global sports star and as such he's now remunerated. He's shined a global spotlight on the sport; his winning personality and phenomenal physical prowess are a unique combination. The way he both engages his fans and is energised by them has helped his popularity escalate to extraordinary levels over the past two years.' The deal moved Bolt to the kind of commercial level already occupied by other sporting figures such as Maria Sharapova, the Russian tennis player who earlier in the year signed an eight-year deal with Nike worth $70 million. He still fell some way short however of the territory occupied by golfer Tiger Woods, whose deal with Nike was reported to be worth $20 million a year.

Bolt also had a book out – entitled *Usain Bolt: 9.58 My Story* – which he boosted with a tour of the UK, taking in appearances on BBC TV and other media outlets. There was a wide and disparate market for it, as the following piece indicates.

Customers wishing to buy crime fiction at the Water-stone's store in Piccadilly this afternoon needed to be unusually patient. One by one they arrived, heading, as perhaps so often before, for the shelves laden with the works of Jeffrey Deaver, Ian Rankin and Patricia Cornwell. One by one their expressions were first bewildered, then thwarted as they were ushered away from the 'event' due to take place just behind a stand marked 'Blue Murder' – a book sign-ing by the global phenomenon known as Usain Bolt. It has to be said that even the mention of the world's fastest man did not instantly disperse the cross looks on some faces. 'Looks frightfully complicated,' announced one well-spoken mum as she ushered her two young children away from the expectant melee of photographers and TV crews corralled in front of the signing desk, and the phalanx of patient visitors, the most enthusiastic of whom had begun queuing outside the door at 6.30 a.m. – five and a half hours before Jamaica's pride and joy was due to arrive. 'We had some people here before I got here at 7.00 a.m.,' said one Waterstone's employee who had seen "em all come and go for book signings over the years: Pele, Bobby Charlton, Lewis Hamilton, Girls Aloud ... This is reaching those numbers,' she added.

The first wave of Bolt fans awaited the signal to advance, many of them clutching copies of the book, *Usain Bolt: 9.58*, with little yellow Post-it notes attached bearing the name which the famed sprinter would be asked to inscribe. Downstairs, another battalion of Bolt lovers stood ready. Outside, further reinforcements had been marshalled into queues that stretched back down Piccadilly and round the corner into Church Place. Right at the back of the queue – again, logically – stood the Last Person In The Queue. It was William, all the way from White-hall. And he knew he was the Last Person In The Queue because the polite store employees had told him so. William was so far back, he didn't even have one of the little grey numbered raffle tickets staff had been handing out all morning. A few places in front of him, a Jamaican gent called Sheldon, sporting a nifty Usain Bolt cap in national colours with those twin peaks of world records emblazoned on it – 9.58, 19.19 – produced his ticket, merely out of the good-ness of his heart. It was number 218.

Back inside, where the people with the smaller numbers stood, you could have cut the tension with a tension cutter – that's if you could ever find a tension cutter. Although why are people always so set on cutting tension? Why can't tension just be left? Anyway. Faces were straining backwards now, towards the stairs, waiting for their Man. Terri, a native of Florida who was staying in London on vacation, was one of several in the queue who had seen details about the signing on Bolt's Facebook site. What a lot of friends this man has. 'I've had a quick look through the book already,' she said. 'It looks a very good read.' June, from Maldon, looked a little preoccupied, but it was fair to assume she was excited inside. 'He's amazing, all the records he sets,' she said. Was it the records, or Bolt's winning personality which had drawn her to Piccadilly on this fine autumnal afternoon? 'It's both really,' she said.

There was a ripple of uncertainty when several men in suits wandered up the stairs very obviously carrying newly bought copies of Tony Blair's new book, *I Was Right*, in the manner of self-conscious fourth-formers who have just discovered Albert Camus or Hunter S. Thompson. Was the former Prime Minister about to stage a rival signing? Well no. The only other signing due that day, an employee explained patiently, would be at 6.00 p.m. Dom Joly. Barely had that bombshell exploded when the patient hordes had their wish.

The Man was here, loping quietly up the stairs as a very British reserve broke out all around him. Wearing a grey hoodie, with the legend: *Usain Bolt …To Da World* – whatever that means – he strode up to the table and produced his trademark Firing The Bow stance for the flickering lightning of the cameras. When the photo-opportunity had finished, and Bolt was allowed to relax the grin he has grinned all over the world in the last couple of years, he sat down at the desk and began the long business of signing with the care of an eager schoolboy. Figures knelt before him, bearing mobile-phone cameras. The Adoration of the Main Guy.

After they had been ushered to, and then away from, the centre of attention, Catherine and Lizzie were detained by the BBC cameras and asked for their impressions of the sprinter. They were happy to repeat their views for insidethegames readers. 'He was nice,' said Catherine. 'He just said, "Have a nice day, hope you didn't have to wait too long ..."'

For these two, Bolt's autograph completed a set. At last month's Diamond League meeting in Crystal Palace, they had got the monikers of Linford Christie and the American who proved back in July that the world and Olympic champion was not unbeatable –Tyson Gay. 'Tyson Gay was really charming,' Lizzie said. 'We thought he might be all moody, but he wasn't like that at all.'

Yasmin Rashid and her friend Raj Patel, two 17-year-old club sprinters from East Grinstead and Crawley respectively, were also pleasantly disposed towards the Signing Man. 'We've seen him run at Crystal Palace, but it was weird to meet him,' Yasmin said. 'He had a very firm handshake,' Raj added. Darna was one of the few present who had met Bolt before – she had ended up sitting near to him last year when she was flying home to London after visiting Jamaica. 'He had some photos taken with me,' she recalled. 'He's still in touch with his roots. He's got time for the people.' As she spoke, Bolt was living up to her words, bent over book number one hundred and whatever with painstaking attention. It was going to be a long session for Usain. A 400 metres of a session ...

Back outside, the queue had advanced. But only marginally. William from Whitehall was still there, hoping...'*

The Bolt brand now engages globally, Whitehall and worldwide. And his feats have already established him as one of sport's all-time greats. He is in the big league. But whereabouts in the big league? How all-time great is he?

In the events at which he excels, the sprints, there are two obvious points of reference in terms of athletics history. They are both Americans, and both, unlike Bolt so far, embraced jumping as well as running in their illustrious careers. They are Jesse Owens and Carl Lewis. Owens could lay claim to fame as a result of just one day in his life – 25 May 1935, when he competed for Ohio State University at Ann Arbor, Michigan. He broke five world records, and equalled a sixth, in the space of just three-quarters of an hour. Despite

---

* Mike Rowbottom, insidethegames.biz, 2 September 2010

suffering from a back pain before his first event, the 100 yards, Owens went on to equal the world record of 9.4 seconds, then raced to the long jump, where he had time for only one attempt. That one attempt saw him become the first man over eight metres, landing at 8.13 metres for a world record that would stand for 25 years. A quarter of an hour later he had the 220 yards flat race, swiftly followed by the 220 yards low hurdles. He won both in world record times, of 20.3 and 22.6 seconds respectively, setting new marks for the 200 metres and 200 metres hurdles en route. That, however, was only part one of the Owens story of glory. A year later, in the intimidating vastness of Berlin's Olympic stadium, he defied the Nazi hierarchy, if not the bulk of a German crowd that afforded him generous applause, to win four gold medals at the 1936 Games – at 100 metres, 200 metres, sprint relay and long jump. For decades, that week's work stood as a benchmark for any athlete aspiring to greatness.

Forty-eight years later, Lewis matched that feat – in medal terms, at least – by collecting golds in the same events at the 1984 Los Angeles Olympics, an achievement that took place to an escalating media fanfare. What Lewis did not have to contend with, however, was the knowledge that he was competing as a guest of a regime whose ideology would have considered him a lesser being on account of the fact that he, like Owens, was black. For all the fact that the German crowd chanted his name with real affection, and for all the undying sportsmanship of his German rival in the long jump, Luz Long, Owens was operating in an inimical environment, which made his feats all the more commendable – and, in the wider scheme of things – all the more valuable. Hitler might not have refused to greet Owens, as the story has it, but Hitler would certainly not have hesitated to shun him had he been in the stadium at a different time. That said, Lewis's career was far longer than that of Owens, or, so far, Bolt's, and it was strewn with medals from start to finish.

Lewis, in fact, began to be named Track and Field Athlete of the Year by *Track and Field News* as early as 1982, and two years later he set the world indoor long jump which stands today. He also won 65 long jumps in a row over a period of a decade. He might have begun his Olympic career in 1980, having qualified for the US team in the long jump and sprint relay, but the US boycott of those Moscow Games meant he had to wait until the home Games four years later to make his big Olympic impact. Even so, the impact of matching Owens's feat, numerically speaking, was diminished by his decision to jump only twice in the long jump, calculating – correctly – that he had done enough to win and need not over-exert himself as he looked to complete his quadruple. The US public made it clear that they had expected him to go all out in his previously stated goal to beat the world record of 8.90 metres which his fellow American Bob Beamon had set in the thin air of Mexico in winning the 1968 Olympic title. Four years later, Lewis secured a second Olympic long jump title, and a second 100 metres title – but only after Ben Johnson's startling world record time of 9.79 seconds had been annulled in the light of his positive doping test. It was not the way Lewis would have wanted to do it, but it was a sixth Olympic title nevertheless.

At the 1992 Barcelona Olympics, Lewis retained his long jump title and, despite not qualifying to run the individual 100 metres, produced one of the most exhilarating sprints ever seen in the anchor relay leg to bring victory to the US – and an eighth Olympic gold to himself. Yet Lewis was still not finished with the Olympics. Four years later, back on home soil in Atlanta, the veteran produced another superbly competitive performance to win a fourth consecutive Olympic long jump title, becoming only the third Olympian to win the same event four times, joining Danish sailor Paul Elvstrom and American discus thrower Al Oerter. In winning a ninth Olympic gold medal, he joined a select group of three others – the flying Finn, Paavo Nurmi, Larissa Latynina and US swimmer Mark Spitz.

And so to the question – where does Bolt rank in all this?

Anyone putting the case for this mighty Jamaican to be placed on the same level as these two American performers would surely point to the measurable impact his performances have had upon the two sprint events. Bolt has obliterated the records at 100 and 200 metres. Although Owens's impact upon the long jump record was profound, he reduced the 100 metres record by one-tenth of a second, from 10.3 to 10.2 seconds, in 1936. Lewis, also a world 100 metres record holder in his time, an electronically timed time, shaved hundredths of seconds off the mark. And despite putting together what is generally regarded even now as the greatest sequence of long jumps in a single competition, at the 1991 IAAF World Championships in Tokyo, Lewis failed in his ambition to eclipse Beamon's world record. That honour fell to another American whose best on that steamy night in Japan was good enough to take both the title and the record as he landed in the sand at 8.95 – Mike Powell. If Powell were to make good on his jocular offer to teach Bolt how to convert all that speed into distance, it is conceivable that the record books would be altered almost 20 years after his own career highlight.

Bolt, however, has indicated on more than one occasion that he is unlikely to turn his mind to long jumping until all his major goals on the track have been achieved. Should he eventually embrace the long jump, rather than attempting to fulfil his childhood longings to be a cricketer, or a footballer, he could yet add a significant element to his already mighty reputation. By his own lights, such a leap of faith, as it were, is only likely to be made after honour has been fully satisfied at 100 and 200 metres. Which, for Bolt, would mean further victories at the 2011 IAAF World Championships, and the following year's Olympics in London. To judge Bolt by factors outside the purely athletic, he seems more akin to Owens than Lewis in terms of the public reaction to him. While Owens was celebrated widely wherever he went, as much for his quiet and humble manner as his sporting ability, Lewis found his long-awaited coming of age in Los Angeles to be undermined by a marked lack of enthusiasm in terms of public impact and commercial response. Lewis's calculating performance in the long jump was not appreciated, and there was also a perception that he was arrogant and aloof, a perception voiced by that most respected of champions, the world and Olympic 400 metres hurdles champion Ed Moses, who accused Lewis of lacking humility.

Coca-Cola, who had offered Lewis a deal before the Games only to be turned down, did not, as might have been expected, renew their offer. He was also dropped by his kit sponsor, Nike. For Lewis, it seemed, winning was far from being everything.

People will compare sporting performances for

as long as there are sporting figures to bring them about. But Bolt, if he is not already in the sporting pantheon, is surely within a couple of years of establishing himself there.

Biography

21 August 1986	Born in Sherwood Content, a small town in the parish of Trelawny, Jamaica where his parents, Wellesley and Jennifer, run the grocery store.
1999	Aged 12, runs 52 seconds flat for 400 metres on a grass track in Manchester, Jamaica.
2001	Aged 14, wins silver medals in his first Caribbean regional event, the CARIFTA Games, Bolt clocking a personal best of 48.28 seconds in the 400 metres and recording 21.81 seconds in the 200 metres.

19 July 2002	At the age of 15, Bolt becomes the youngest winner of a World Junior title, taking gold in the 200 metres and silver in both the 4×100 metres and 4×400 metres relays. The event is held in his home capital of Kingston.
2003	Transfers from Trelawny to begin training at the University of Technology, Kingston.
9–13 July 2003	Wins gold in the 200 metres at World Youth Championships in Sherbrooke, Canada.
18–20 July 2003	Equals Roy Martin's World Junior 200 metres record of 20.13 seconds in winning at the Pan American Junior Championships.
23–31 August 2003	Misses World Championships in Paris after conjunctivitis disrupts his training.
2004	Turns professional under coaching guidance of Fitz Coleman.

9–11 April 2004	Becomes first junior to break the 20-second mark in the 200 metres, clocking 19.93 seconds at the CARIFTA Games in Bermuda.
24 August 2004	Exits in the first round of the 200 metres at the 2004 Athens Olympics, hampered by injury. Glen Mills takes over as Bolt's coach.
8–11 July 2005	Claims gold medal in the 200 metres at the Central American and Caribbean Championships with a time of 20.03 seconds.
11 August 2005	At World Championships in Helsinki drops out of contention halfway through 200 metres final because of injury and finishes last in 26.27 seconds.
19 November 2005	Sustains minor facial injuries after his Honda Accord car was in collision with another vehicle in Kingston.
March 2006	Hamstring injury forces him to miss Commonwealth Games in Melbourne.

10 September 2006	Takes bronze in IAAF World Athletics final in Stuttgart.
25 June 2007	Breaks Don Quarrie's Jamaican 200 metres record of 19.86 seconds at the National Championships, clocking 19.75 seconds. In return, Mills allows him to run a serious 100 metres in Crete, where he wins in 10.03 seconds.
30 August 2007	Wins 200 metres silver at World Championships in Osaka, and also wins silver as a member of the 4×100 metres relay.
3 May 2008	Runs the second fastest 100 metres time in history at the Jamaica Invitational, clocking 9.76 seconds.
31 May 2008	Breaks the world record in the 100 metres at the Reebok Grand Prix in New York, beating a field including world champion Tyson Gay to record 9.72 seconds in only his fifth race over the distance.

13 July 2008	Beats his personal best in the 200 metres, finishing in 19.67 seconds in Athens to register the fastest time over the distance in 2008 and the fifth fastest 200 metres time ever.
16 August 2008	Wins 100 metres gold at the Beijing Olympics, lowering his world record to 9.69 seconds.
20 August 2008	Completes Olympic sprint double, winning the 200 metres in world record time of 19.30 seconds, 0.02 seconds inside the mark set by Michael Johnson in winning the 1996 Olympic title in Atlanta.
22 August 2008	Runs third leg as Jamaica earns Olympic 4×100 metres relay victory in world record time of 37.10 seconds.
23 August 2008	Voted IAAF World Male Athlete of the Year.
29 April 2009	Escapes serious injury when his BMW M3 car skids off road outside of Kingston and overturns. Requires minor foot surgery.

17 May 2009	Wins Manchester Great City Games 1500 metres in world best time of 14.35 seconds, covering first 100 metres in 9.91 seconds and last 100 metres with flying start in 8.70 seconds.
10 June 2009	Wins 2009 Laureus World Sportsman of the Year.
20 August 2009	Claims second gold medal at World Championships, lowering his 200 metres world record to 19.19 seconds.
1 May 2010	Opens season by winning 200 metres at Jamaica National Championships in 19.56 seconds, which remains the fastest time run all year.
19 May 2010	Wins 100 metres in Daegu, venue for the IAAF World Championships in 2011, in 9.86 seconds.
23 May 2010	Wins 200 metres at IAAF Samsung Diamond League meeting in Shanghai, in 19.76.

27 May 2010	Wins 300 metres at Golden Spike meeting in Ostrava in 30.97 seconds, the second fastest time ever recorded, in rainy conditions. Suffers Achilles tendon injury which forces him to miss scheduled appearance at New York's Diamond League meeting.
8 July 2010	Returns to action at the Lausanne Diamond League meeting, winning the 100 metres in 9.82 seconds, which equals the fastest time yet run in the season by his fellow Jamaican, Asafa Powell.
16 July 2010	Beats Powell in the Paris Diamond League meeting in Saint Denis, winning the 100 metres in 9.84.
6 August 2010	Suffers his first defeat in two years at the Stockholm Diamond League meeting, where he is beaten by Tyson Gay. The American clocks 9.84 seconds, with Bolt second in 9.97.
10 August 2010	Bolt announces he is finishing his season early as a precaution in order not to exacerbate a longstanding problem with his lower back.

24 August 2010	Signs new deal with sports manufacturer Puma, billed as 'by far the largest ever given to a track and field athlete' and thought to be worth £10m over three years.
September 2010	Tours UK and Australia promoting his new book *Usain Bolt: 9.58 My Story* (HarperSport).

Acknowledgements

Kelly Holmes: thank you for the time and care you have put into producing the foreword to this book. It is greatly appreciated.

I would like to thank the *Guardian* and the *Observer* newspapers for allowing me to use material originally published by their writers, notably Donald McRae and Anna Kessel, whose additional insights have been invaluable.

I am also very grateful to Patrick Robinson for his kindness in allowing me to quote extensively from his excellent book, *Jamaican Athletics: A Model for 2012 and the World* (BlackAmber, 2007).

Thanks go also to Duncan and Sarah at insidethegames.biz for allowing use of material I have written for the site, and to my sometime colleagues at the International Association of Athletics Federations, Chris Turner, Bob Ramsak and Dave Martin, for all their assistance and input.

Finally my thanks go to my wife, Tig, for bearing with me during what has been, at times, a faintly fraught process. Sorry!

JAMAICAN ATHLETICS
A MODEL FOR 2012 AND THE WORLD
Patrick Robinson

The book celebrates an area of excellence in Jamaica that deservedly brings pride to every Jamaican, and excites wonder and curiosity in others – the country's high quality performance in global athletics over the past sixty years; during that time Jamaica has frequently placed between third and tenth in athletics at the Olympic Games and the World Athletics Championships. At the Beijing Olympics from a field of 205 countries, Jamaica placed third in track and field athletics. This is an achievement that is wholly disproportionate to Jamaica's size and resources. The book, which has a chapter on Jamaica's triumph in Beijing, seeks to isolate the environment in which the athletic product of excellence thrives. It asserts that the environment consists of the rich legacy and history of athletics in Jamaica, the innate competitive, assertive and resilient spirit that is native to Jamaicans, the immense athletic talent that abounds in the country, and, most important, the systemic and structural features that underpin the junior and senior athletic programmes. The book offers an explanation and analysis of the athletic system, praising, in particular, the quality of the coaching, and the intensity of the training regimen in the junior programme, which, it argues, is the best in the world.

It is suggested that the Jamaican product is a model for the world, particularly developing countries, because it illustrates how success in athletics can be achieved at the global level with relatively little resources. Attention is paid to the features of the athletic system that may readily be replicated in other countries.

978 1 906413 29 3

£12.99

BARACK OBAMA:
THE MOVEMENT FOR CHANGE
Anthony Painter

Every now and again America confronts its demons, walks away from deep internal division, and strives towards justice.

Barack Obama: The Movement for Change tells the story of a visionary leader who refuses to be limited by America's history and determines instead to change it. His plan for change is the latest expression of a movement for justice: a movement that has swept forward with the collective energy of great leaders like Martin Luther King, Robert Kennedy, Lyndon B. Johnson, Harold Washington, Chicago's first black mayor, and countless others who have bent the 'arc of morality' towards justice.

By looking at the biography of the man, this mixed-race Hawaiian with Kenyan and Kansas parents, a window on America in the twenty-first century is revealed. His life touches and is touched by a sinking community on Chicago's South Side. He challenges the lazy assumptions of American racial discourse. He creates an argument for political change and a different America. He wins a presidential election few thought possible when his formidable campaign was launched.

Barack Obama: The Movement for Change tells a story for our times. It is not the story of a single man. It is the story of a movement and of the people who drove the movement forward. It is a new American story that will cascade down the generations. America has changed and Barack Obama's story tells us how and why and what we can expect.

978 1 906413 23 1
£6.99

BILL MORRIS:
A TRADE UNION MIRACLE
Geoffrey Goodman

LORD MORRIS OF HANDSWORTH OJ is the first black man to rise to the top of any major British institution. When, in 1992, he became general secretary of the Transport and General Workers Union – then the largest trade union in the country – it marked a huge break in the culture of British working-class attitudes towards racial discrimination. The first black immigrant to join the governing board of the Bank of England; the first black immigrant to become president of the Trades Union Congress ... he was, as he says in this book, 'always a first' in this respect.

This is the story of his rise to the top of British public life after arriving in Birmingham in the mid-1950s, aged 16, to join his mother who had come to England a short time earlier. Bill Morris was born and brought up in a small rural village about sixty miles from the Jamaican capital, Kingston. As a child his overwhelming ambition was to become a professional cricketer and play for the West Indies; he has had to put up with what he regards as the lesser honour of sitting on the England and Wales Cricket Board at Lord's. His story is a fascinating account of a unique rise from the shop floor to international status.

Praise for *From Bevan to Blair*:

'What Geoffrey Goodman doesn't know about political journalism didn't happen. This fascinating book takes us through the pass door to the corridors of power'

Keith Waterhouse

'Through [the] momentous years in Labour history, indeed Bristish history, Geoffrey Goodman has had a special ringside seat. We all knew he had the best story to tell and here it is. It is a triumph of character as much as journalistic skill'

Michael Foot

978 1 906413 42 2
£6.99

NAVI PILLAY:
REALISING HUMAN RIGHTS FOR ALL
Sam Naidu

In September 2008 Navi Pillay was appointed UN High Commissioner for Human Rights.

Pillay, a trailblazer in Human Rights law, was born in 1941 to a humble Indian family in apartheid South Africa. She faced enormous obstacles to her aspirations for further education and a meaningful career. However, in 1967 she was the first black woman in South Africa to set up a law practice, which she used to defend many anti-apartheid activists. She also used her skills to protect the rights of political prisoners and remarkably, in 1973, she succeeded in obtaining legal representation and basic amenities for the inmates of Robben Island. In 1995 when the first democratic government was formed in South Africa, Nelson Mandela nominated Pillay as the first black female judge in the Supreme Court. In the same year she joined the International Criminal Tribunal for Rwanda. Since then Pillay has become one of the world's leading advocates in the field of Human Rights.

No. 64 Navi Pillay
The 100 Most Powerful Women in the World
Forbes magazine, 19 August 2009

'I have heard so much about Navi Pillay and was excited to meet her'
Jane Fonda

'Her extraordinary life'
BBC *Woman's Hour*

978 1 906413 45 3
£6.99

CARLOS ACOSTA:
THE RELUCTANT DANCER
Margaret Willis

Carlos Acosta grew up in a cramped apartment in Cuba, knowing poverty, hardship and family tragedies. He roamed the streets barefoot when he should have been in school, stole fruit from neighbours' orchards, and wanted nothing more than to be a footballer like any other young boy. His father, however, fearing for his future, enrolled him in ballet school where he would be disciplined, trained for a career, and fed. It was many years before the young Carlos would accept the strict demands of a pursuit he saw as 'sissy'.

Today Carlos Acosta is one of the world's most stunning classical ballet dancers, admired for his firecracker, yet refined technique, for his riveting acting and for his magnetic presence on stage. He is considered a national treasure in his own country, and a matinee idol to global dance goers. *The Reluctant Dancer* charts the trajectory of this exceptional ballet maverick who has captured the hearts of audiences worldwide.

'One of the most brilliant male ballet dancers in the world today'
Sunday Times

'There is, without fail, a collective intake of breath when Carlos Acosta leaps on stage'
Evening Standard

'Acosta, strong and sexy, the ultimate alpha male, offers virile dance of force and finesse'
The Times

'He comes so close to the footlights, you feel he wants to break their bounds and bring the audience onto the stage'
Daily Telegraph

978 1 906413 71 2
£6.99